HAUNTED BY THE ABYSS

The Otherworldly Experiences
of Paranormal Sarah

SARAH
SODERLUND

Llewellyn Worldwide
Woodbury, Minnesota

Photo by Sophia Helen Photography

About the Author

Sarah Soderlund (Minneapolis, MN) is a psychic and paranormal investigator. She has studied parapsychology at the University of Edinburgh, holds a master's degree in forensic psychology, and is pursuing a doctorate. Sarah hosts the *Skeleton Key*, a weekly Internet radio show, gives presentations at various paranormal conferences across the U.S., and has appeared on many paranormal radio programs.

To Write the Author

If you wish to contact the author or would like more information about this book, please write to the author in care of Llewellyn Worldwide, and we will forward your request. Both the author and publisher appreciate hearing from you and learning of your enjoyment of this book and how it has helped you. Llewellyn Worldwide cannot guarantee that every letter written to the author can be answered, but all will be forwarded. Please write to:

Sarah Soderlund
℅ Llewellyn Worldwide
2143 Wooddale Drive
Woodbury, MN 55125-2989

Please enclose a self-addressed stamped envelope for reply,
or $1.00 to cover costs. If outside the USA, enclose
an international postal reply coupon.

To my dear family and support system
who have taken a journey on this wild spiritual
ride for which there is no exit. I could not begin
to find peace or serenity amidst the evil of the world
if I did not have the blessing of my husband
Brandon and my two dear sons.

FIRST EDITION
First Printing, 2015

Book design by Bob Gaul
Cover images by iStockphoto.com/27753635/©tanys04
                iStockphoto.com/7608407/©logoff
Cover design by Ellen Lawson
Editing by Patti Frazee

Llewellyn Publications is a registered trademark of Llewellyn Worldwide Ltd.

Library of Congress Cataloging-in-Publication Data
Soderlund, Sarah, 1984–
  Haunted by the abyss: the otherworldly experiences of paranormal Sarah
  Sarah Soderlund.—First Edition.
     pages cm
  ISBN 978-0-7387-4589-3
1. Soderlund, Sarah, 1984– 2. Parapsychology—Biography. 3. Occultism—
Biography. I. Title.
  BF1027.S665A3 2015
  133.9'1092—dc23 [B]
                            2015022998

Llewellyn Publications
A Division of Llewellyn Worldwide Ltd.
2143 Wooddale Drive
Woodbury, MN 55125-2989
www.llewellyn.com

Printed in the United States of America

Contents

Foreword

Think back to your childhood when everything was new and exciting and every day promised a new adventure and new explorations. There were nights when your parents or a loved one would tell you a scary story before tucking you tightly in your covers, making sure to leave the nightlight on and close that closet door—just in case some imaginary monster might slip through.

Many of us have memories like that, and as we grow older the scary stories become simple little anecdotes of our childhood, simple little memories, and as we walk past our closet door during adulthood we don't think twice about whether or not it's open a crack, and we don't worry that a little nightlight isn't plugged into the wall outlet.

But what if your childhood were different? What if the scary stories weren't comical and the ghost in the closet *wasn't* imaginary?

At night before tucking me into bed in the tiny spare room in the "scary" attic, my grandmother used to tell a very "scary" story about a tiny woman who lived far away in the land of the Giants. The lady found a toe bone from one of the Giants and, being very poor, made a soup from it. One of the Giants came to retrieve it, and every night he would stomp and yell outside her house, "Give me back my bone! Give me back my toe!" As a child this story seemed mildly scary, but it was mostly funny.

Why didn't stories like the Giant's toe bone scare me? Because I had already seen and heard things that were much scarier. I knew there were things I couldn't explain and that I didn't understand. Now don't get me wrong—anybody who knew me as a child will tell you that I had a vivid imagination. If my mother was still alive she'd be happy to tell you stories about my sister's imaginary friend who was simply named "Boy." I made a huge fuss if Mom did not set a place for him at the table or hold the car door open long enough for him to get in. I made sure that Boy got to go everywhere that we went and always had a chair to sit in or toys to play with or a cup to drink from.

But I knew the difference between Boy and the things that I saw at night. Today at this point of my life, I can tell you now that I have seen and heard and even *felt* things that some people would probably never believe. I'm okay with that. I was raised in a Southern Baptist household and tried very hard to hang onto that as long as possible, but when it did not explain the experiences I was having or my psychic abilities whenever they started to really come into bloom, I had a conflict of interest and was forced to find my own way.

The hardest thing about the paranormal, the supernatural, and things beyond this realm is that you have either experienced them or you haven't. If you have experienced them, you are likely a "believer" at some level, from the curious Psychic Fair attendee to the spiritual practitioner. If you haven't experienced anything, you likely write it all off as hokum. Sounds like a silly axiom, doesn't it? But these phenomena are around us all the time, whether you are a believer or a skeptic.

My husband has never had a paranormal experience. He appreciates what I do in my work and he respects my privacy and my space, and he even participates once in a while in an investigation just to see what it's like. But in his heart of hearts, he doesn't really have the same depth of belief that I do. Those who have experienced something at least have a curiosity: they want to know more, they want to know why, they want to know what, and they want to know how. They want to explain their experience, to figure out how to put it in logical terms, how to put it into a little box so that they can open it up, take out and read a manual, and understand every little detail. Then you have the other extreme: people like myself who are spiritual practitioners and paranormal investigators and counselors who understand that sometimes you cannot put these things in a box. You cannot explain them with a set of rules and guidelines. You have to understand that they are amorphous and it's a matter of perspective and beliefs.

But nowhere along the way will I say that these events and these phenomena in these circumstances do not exist. They're not the fabrications of imagination, or hyper-activated brain-induced visions. Science has even proven that you can have paranormal phenomenon occur similarly to different people at the same time and they will describe it exactly the same even if they're a world apart from each other.

So here is where I ask you, the reader, to stop for a moment. Are you the skeptic who has never heard a bump in the night that you couldn't explain, or seen a ghostly figure walk across your bedroom late at night, or been driving down the highway and seen a black figure run across the road and you swerve to not hit it and find that there's really nothing there? Are you the believer: the Spiritualist looking to learn more, looking to hear another person's perspective on their experience in the world of the paranormal? Or are you that person just barely curious; just opening that box for the first time wondering what, where, when, how, and is this possible?

I tell you no matter which category you fit into—YES these events happen, YES these phenomena are possible, YES the circumstances do occur. I implore you to open your mind as you read these stories and these recollections. Try not to use your logical little box. Throw it away. Put it to the side. Let these perspectives come to you in their ambiguous, amorphous forms and just soak them in, and listen to find out how it applies to and affects you.

Do you have anything in common with any of these experiences? Have you seen anything similar in your own life? You might be able to learn from another person's experience and another person's lifetime. All you have to do is throw out the rule book for these few pages and just open up your mind. Open up the child part of yourself that's still nestled tightly in the covers as that loved one is telling you a ghost story. Listen to these tales that one person went through and then ask yourself: Is this for real? Or do you choose to keep that ghost hidden in the closet; the nightlight turned on brightly as you sleep? It's all a matter of perspective. We all have one.

After you finish this book I hope—I urge—those of you who are skeptics to put that box of logic aside … and try to change your perspective.

Cat Wilder
Author, Psychic, Spiritual Practitioner,
Egyptian Divination Specialist, Energy Healer

"When you look into an abyss,
the abyss also looks into you."
—Friedrich Nietzsche—

Introduction

The paranormal has been part of my life for so long—the veil almost begins at birth. The veil is a term used to describe the metaphysical curtain that closes the physical world off to the mysteries of whatever happens after you die. I think for most, their first paranormal experience is what leads them into the adventure of the mysterious and they have a distinct delineation of the "before and after" of when the paranormal became part of their life.

Sometimes I wish I had a time before the paranormal, but in truth, my life has always been a little paranormal and a lot strange. I've tried to push my memory back as far as it will go, into the dark folds of where I begin to wonder whether my experiences were imagination or whether they were reality.

For me, those two terms—imagination and reality—have always been a little intermingled, and I think sometimes it's a defense mechanism to just believe what you're experiencing might be something crawling up from the depths of your mind. We all have nightmares, scary movies that linger beyond the film reel, and even a little anxiety about a particular incident that seems to haunt us. I always tell my clients, those who turn to me for my experience in the paranormal field and in psychology of the paranormal, to ask themselves where their fear began.

I encourage those who experience the paranormal to be skeptical, logical, rational, even when the experience doesn't seem to fit into the real world. I know this can be a difficult task to accomplish because of the conflict I face every day trying to do it. Take each new experience from day to day and do not let fear pollute your decisions. It is important to understand the difference between the fear that is an evolutionary response to something that puts us in danger, and the fear that seems to come from nowhere. When you remove the fear, you see the paranormal as uncharted territory. Just as some might have been fearful of a man landing on the moon, you can begin to see your paranormal experience as a possible leap for mankind.

So where does my story begin? In the following pages you will find chapters, little snippets of memories that I can recall being specific and particular incidents that ring true in my mind. Some researchers believe that our memory tends to recall and imprint traumatic experiences more than positive growth opportunities. From my experience, I would have to agree with this, as most of my memories seem to erupt from the shadows and my past. The truth is, ever since I was a young girl I have experienced strange phenomena on a minute-to-minute, day-to-day, week-to-week, person-to-person basis.

It is important for children to feel a sense of security. Aside from my experiences as an abused child, having spiritual occurrences happening on a daily basis was stressful. I remember seeing images of death, mangled bodies, limbless apparitions, and getting playbacks and psychic visions of memories that were not my own as a child. That is how my psychic experiences began. At first I thought I was simply exaggerating my imagination. At a young age, though, you do begin to realize the difference between pretending to be at a tea party and actually being at dinner.

After my friends would go home and the toys were put away, my tea parties still had guests that were uninvited. It seemed as though I had to become desensitized to seeing these dark images, these unwanted figures, and I had to learn to enjoy life despite the stress. Thanks to my experience growing up in a haunted house with spiritual phenomena, I already knew how to deal with these issues.

I also think that being a skeptic (skeptic meaning someone who has a questioning attitude) has helped me to remain sane and stress-free despite the bombardment of paranormal phenomenon. Being someone desperately trying to cling to the scientific community where things seem more real, stable, accepted, and unquestionable, going into psychology would somehow help me identify with what everyone else thought was a problem: mental stress. My entire lifestyle and perspective on life is seen through a very taboo filter. I cannot simply share an elevator with just anyone and open up about the work I do and the experiences I have had in the paranormal without some concern I might be seen as a crazy woman. Because so many skeptics and individuals working in the scientific field would discredit a paranormal experience to mental health, I set out to understand mental health. After my personal experiences and now my formal education in psychology, I can definitely say that paranormal phenomenon exists outside the realm of mental illness.

I suppose the reason I went into forensic psychology is because I desperately want to understand how one person's experience on this planet can be so dramatically different from another's. I can empathize with those clients who have a strange happening and reach out to their peers for advice only to be met with ridicule. I can also empathize with those clients who experience fear in the safety of their own home and try to discover new ways to cope with the unexplained.

Forensic psychology was unique because it not only explored the psychology of the mind but also because it also explores why heinous crime and unthinkable acts are being committed. Often, seeing things that cannot be unseen and learning to detach from reality is the best piece of advice those working in the field can give.

Paranormal Sarah

For those reading this book and who are unfamiliar with my background in the paranormal community, I was given the nickname "Paranormal Sarah" in 2008. Big names in the field, personalities featured on television shows worldwide, and radio hosts for paranormal broadcasts all use this nickname and it has since stuck. Despite my opinion, I was always introduced as "Paranormal Sarah" at events and conventions, and it somehow made me memorable. Working with popular television networks has allowed me to travel the world, and I have been to more than twelve countries to explore haunted locations such as the London Tower, concentration camps in Germany, and the catacombs of France.

My formal education is in forensic psychology, for which I am pursuing my doctorate degree; I am also a licensed hypnotherapist and holistic practitioner. When it comes to my research associated with the Parapsychological Association and Mutual UFO Network (M.U.F.O.N.) and similar affiliations, it focuses on clients who are recovering from extreme paranormal cases including but not limited to: alien abduction, poltergeist, pre- and post-exorcism, incubus, succubus, night terrors, and other unexplained happenings that lead to extreme anxiety disorders. I am utilizing my education and experience to help others who are experiencing paranormal phenomenon.

I hope that some of my experiences prove to be not only an entertaining read for those of you giving your time and energy to my story, but also that this book can be a learning tool. If not to provide an empathetic shoulder for those experiencing scary and traumatic events, perhaps it can also be a tool to help give you insight into what growing up with paranormal phenomena can be like.

ONE

Our Haunted House

Having a psychic experience, a spiritual awakening, or experiencing a haunting in your home defies the current laws of science and can make your entire world feel a little unstable. For those who are religious, paranormal occurrences might be met with answers leading you to demons, angels, and the process of an exorcism. If you don't find sanctuary in your faith and religion suddenly the world crumbles, because what else could be going on? Things are walking through walls! You find yourself resorting to crazy things, considering ridiculous options, and some days questioning your sanity.

I thought by immersing myself with those people who are labeled as crazy and psychotic I might see the clear line between what reason and sanity really is. Where does logic and rational thought break into imagination? I have found through my personal experience in a haunted house, traveling the world to some of the scariest places on earth, and working with some of the most mentally ill people in the nation, that reality and fear are subjective no matter the situation at hand.

My experience and my education have both lent themselves as useful tools to me within the paranormal community, not just as someone who currently lives with unique and unexplained phenomenon, but also for someone who helps others experiencing the same. I have found refuge in knowing I can help others and also in knowing that there is much to be discovered in this loose community we call the paranormal field.

Before I delve into my firsthand accounts, it is appropriate to introduce my family and support system, and also the biggest influences within my experiences in the paranormal. My parents played a large role in how I view the unexplained. My father was always a hard-working man of few words. He was raised in a home among many brothers and sisters with educated parents who immersed themselves deeply in the Southern Baptist Church. Church wasn't just something you went to on Sunday, but was found in your heart and home. Scripture led almost every conversation in the household and always every scolding.

My father's parents were a great influence in my life, and their love for Jesus Christ and scripture always gave me some sort of faith that there was something good to be found in organized religion. My grandparents were humble, genuine, and kind. I swear the line never ended at my grandfather's funeral when people came to pay their respects and share stories of his kind heart. They dedicated their life to the church and they believed in it. I associated the church to being like another person in the family. Religion provided consequence, rules, guidance, and did its best to tell imaginative stories to explain all my childhood questions of life.

My mother, a fiery redhead and crass woman who spoke openly, was also raised in a religious household. Quick-witted, she often spoke out of turn; she found herself the rebel of her family and community. She was a cheerleader, a student council member, popular with the boys, and a mischievous sibling.

Though she agreed with my father that organized religion was important, especially for instilling good values, she was also a very holistic woman. My mother always stepped to the beat of her own drum, and if her opinion conflicted with the Bible she'd assumed she was right. "The Bible was written by a bunch of old men anyway," she would often hiss. My mother valued the spirit of nature above all and was happiest when she was outside or playing music. My mother taught me how to harmonize, how to sit at the table, how to plant seeds, how to smile on stage, and, most importantly, "It's easier to ask forgiveness than to ask permission."

My mother divorced my father and regretted the decision until the day she died. She died from long-term alcohol abuse and liver failure in the year 2012, just two weeks after the birth of my first son, her first grandchild. She was in her early fifties and also planned her own funeral.

My sister, eight years older than I, joined me in the garden with our parents as we grew our food, raised many animals, and denied popular medicine in most cases. My sister was always chasing some cat around the yard, or had her nose stuck in a fantasy novel, or was making cassette tapes of her favorite bands for me. Though my sister had always been private about her space and, as sisters often do, we fought constantly, we also shared a deep joy in exploring the paranormal together.

My sister would build haunted houses in her room and dare me to enter. My sister also always encouraged me to find the answer and read a book. If I ever had a question about anything at all, my sister would help me find the answer. To this day, if I have a question about anything within the paranormal I often turn to her first.

In her teenage years, my sister defied Christianity and explored more natural religions such as Paganism and Wicca. She joined me at some of Kansas City's best psychic conventions and investigations and encouraged me to find my own way. She now works as a gifted animal communicator and psychic medium who specializes in Egyptian theology. She is a Priestess of Sekhmet and counsels people with unique spirituality.

Our parents may have been strict, but they had many friends from various backgrounds who often joined us at the dinner table. A close neighbor was a Cherokee Indian who shared his heritage with my mom's side of the family, and they both found great pleasure in stone collecting, music therapy, recreational drugs, and talking with the spirit world.

My mother, my mother's mother, and my sister were all very open to their psychic abilities and sharp intuition. They would garden by the moon, share a spell or two at least once a day on some superstition or stressor, and often spoke out loud about their spirituality. I remember my mother always teaching me that food was medicine, and she is the person who initially inspired my suspicion of pharmaceuticals.

My grandma, mother, and sister could always say who was calling on the phone long before caller ID existed. They did very well at the dog races, had precognitive dreams, and always seemed overly empathetic.

Though my father could never deny the presence of intuition in our household, he preferred to agree with his parents that meddling with the spirit world could never do any good. He was a stern religious man who trusted only in God.

My sister later became a great teacher for me. Some of my first experiences with divination, paranormal investigation, and communicating with the dead were all instigated by the passion my sister had for spirituality and the afterlife. I remember our grandmother explaining how to use daily playing cards as prayer tools. My mother insisted we profile the world around us at all times. Most likely as an intuitive mother to her children, she taught us to be trust our gut reactions when we were suspicious of others. My talents of handwriting analysis, phrenology, palm reading, and profiling all stem from the daily utterances of how to read people, according to my mother.

Since our childhood, my sister and I have been on countless paranormal investigations together, have lectured and performed psychic readings at events all across the nation, and have done many workshops in tandem for others and their abilities. From dream interpretation workshops to psychic readings for clients, we have learned how to use the strengths of each other to learn the most from the experience at hand.

I vividly remember it was the year 1998 when my sister and I joined the Physical Research Society of Kansas City, Missouri. Our paranormal encounters went from being something homebound to something we could share with others in our community. It was through workshops, organizations like M.U.F.O.N., and even private groups that we knew we were not alone in being alienated from our peers, and that we weren't completely crazy after all.

It is hard to believe that I had such a religious childhood—I was even a guidance counselor at a Christian camp summer after summer—and yet be someone who does active research in the parapsychology community today. The truth is, the books and articles I publish, the lectures I give, and the research I continue to do are not only a journey of self-help and spiritual growth, but in some way serve a greater purpose as well. For that reason, I know my learning will never be complete and the veil will never close.

The House Might Be Alive

What makes a house haunted, really? Some believe it's the land the house resides upon. Well, if that's the case then I guess Kansas City, Missouri, is no different than any other Midwest town for having great roots in a Native American culture full of remorse, trauma, and violence. It all resided here: mystery and skepticism, faith, the supernatural, cultural figureheads ranging from Billy the Kid to Sacajawea.

Parkville, Missouri, is a small town in the northern suburbs of Kansas City. On the Missouri side of the Missouri River, the town itself has history with the Civil War, the border war, Indian and slave trade, adventures on the Lewis and Clark trail, and even public hangings of the Japanese during the recent world wars. Indian tribes lost their homes and were relocated, slavery ran rampant off the Kansas City ports, and bushwhackers fought the Jayhawks no less than two-hundred-some years ago.

Perhaps the land was haunted, perhaps not. I personally believe that a haunting is an imprint: a cluster of charged energy, a traumatic event, unrestful spirit, a story to be told. A haunting can mean a person or an event in history. For that reason, I do believe that the land can be haunted. I believe that in a location where murder or even war is inflicted, spirits group together like teenagers in the locker room whispering about the events at hand.

One of my best experiences with haunted areas of land would be Gettysburg, Pennsylvania, where you can walk out on the misty battlefields and hear gunshots. I believe a house can be haunted. I believe a person can be haunted. I believe I have been haunted.

We always knew of the presence of the strange old woman who lived in my childhood home before we had ever lived there. She never really left the house at all, though she had indeed died. My mother said when they found the small property the walls had been covered with bits and pieces of wallpaper and newspaper tattered and torn into a strange pattern.

The old woman had emptied her vacuum cleaner, and the clutter of her home, out over the front porch and left it in a heaping, organized pile of trash upon the yard. The house was small, adorned with shag carpet so commonly found in the '70s. Its best feature was the two-and-a-half acres of plush land it sat upon.

Now, every house has its creeks and cracks, but our house, our haunted house, had just a little more than usual.

Growing up with my mother and sister meant that when I had a scary nightmare or saw someone in the corner it wasn't always assumed that I had imagined it. Instead, my mother or sister would ask me open-ended questions about what exactly I had experienced. If I insisted there was someone in the living room talking to me they would ask, "What do they look like?"; "Why are they here?"; "Do you know them?" Asking these questions allowed me to validate my visions, it kept the spirits coming, and I didn't associate fear with the experiences.

From the very beginning, it never occurred to me that I might just be imagining something, but instead all of my experiences were treated as very real phenomena. It was only later in my childhood when I undoubtedly knew these occurrences were real that I realized just why my sister and mother responded the way they did. If I felt something brush the back of my hair while in the shower, it was normal. To hear someone walk down the hallway at night just before falling asleep and gently open the door as if to check on me, though I knew no one was there and no one was up, was a very normal occurrence. Having the cupboards open on their own, a glass move across the table, or a book fly off the shelf just as I was talking about it was something, again, all too normal and very common in our haunted house.

It wasn't until I was older, around the age of five or six, that I visited the homes of my friends and realized not everybody had a house as interactive as mine. Our home always felt alive. My sister's friends, who would come to stay at night and wake up in the evening hours screaming out of their sleeping bags, initiated the thought that maybe our house was unique; we realized just how unnatural our house really was. Someone was always listening; the reflection wasn't the only thing watching you back, and usually it wasn't your imagination.

Though it might sound scary to some, and it was definitely scary to those who were a guest in our home on occasion, growing up with an active knowledge of the afterlife actually gave me more faith in my religion. It wasn't hard to believe that we went somewhere when our body died and that we could interact with our loved ones well after we were dead when we had people who interacted with us every day that clearly were not from the physical world. It wasn't always scary, we gave the spirits rules and guidelines, and eventually we kind of always knew we were never alone, which became a spiritual comfort in a sense. I've never really had a fear of death and I've never really had the anxiety of what might happen if my religion were wrong, and I owe that in part to those spirits I grew up with in our haunted house. They became part of my family and my baseline.

Why So Scary?

My husband has yet to have a valid paranormal experience that has teetered his skepticism to "belief." We are both anxiously waiting for the magic number to be reached for which the late-night dish crashing can go from "coincidence" to "possible something." He has experienced my psychic phenomenon and has heard countless firsthand testimonials but struggles to differentiate intuition from psychic gift. Because he is an open-minded man, and because he yearns to connect with me in some way on the spiritual realm, he is always encouraging me to share my paranormal phenomena and is open to exploring the unknown along with me. The waiting game will hopefully soon become an experience.

Meanwhile, we wait. He does not believe demonic energies or "attachments" exist and is convinced that if indeed there is some amount of our consciousness that transcends the physical body's death, then why is it resentful? "It doesn't make sense and only really reflects our fear of lack of control, the lack of power. We cannot control death, we cannot experience death and the greatest evil to happen to us is death; which is the believed intention of a demon. Why though would an energy, a vulgar intention, come into play? Demons, takers of death, only appear to those who fear death. Religions don't keep you safe or give you faith, they fill you with anxiety and judgment. The wise man knows not to fear death and therefore has no fear of a personified analogy of a creature that can take it away…" Our philosophy goes on late into the night.

"Other than anticipation, death is coming and we cannot predict or control that. We can both wither away and worry or we can live. Those risk takers, those happy-despite-obstacles people, those without fear ironically seem to live the longest and most 'meaningful' lives and they would say they're spiritual more than religious. Demons don't exist to those people who live to live."

I suppose in some ways I agree with him that when the anxiety and fear associated with death is gone then the motivations put in place by any "demonic entity" are completely removed. When you have that release, that acceptance, then you are set free to walk in the valley of the shadow of death and fear no evil. A peace that most do not come to until their dying day and others never feel at all.

I suppose I saw scary images, restless spirits, and associated an anxiety about life. These people weren't demonic, they were unhappy, and therefore were restless searching for something greater. I don't want to live my life haunting a dream, restlessly searching; I want to live.

What Else Is Haunted?

If a haunting is not created by the land or the history of the home, researchers in the paranormal field might suggest a haunting has to do with the proximity to a ley line, a river source, limestone, or even to a religious location. Parkville, Missouri, is home to all of those factors, and though my childhood home was not made of limestone—it was just an early 1930s wooden structure on a cement foundation—strange occurrences took place nonetheless. The home was small. There was a cement patio adorned with white pillars and it had a wooden porch swing. The screen door led to a small living room that initially didn't even have a television. The dining room viewed through to the living room and the kitchen was attached to the back of the home with a small back door that opened to the remaining acreage decorated in large oak trees. Three small bedrooms were off the back east side of the house, just beyond the living room. Cracked moldings traced the ceiling like a white-trash gingerbread house made with wet icing. Each room was glued to the next and showing age. The home was unique and delicate.

In the early '80s, when I was just five years old, my bedroom was painted bright yellow with a shag green carpet and was found at the end of the hall facing the bedroom door to my parents' sanctuary. The square room had one wall with a large window staring out into the backyard, another large window facing our driveway, a wall of shelving and the entrance to my room, and lastly, a wall made up of a small closet. It was a tightly packed room at the end of the hall. I remember how big it always seemed growing up. Even though the house has been remodeled, it still sits on the original foundation. When I go there now, I can nearly touch each wall with my fingertips when stretching my body out. But then, as a small girl of only five years old, the room seemed vast and terribly hard to keep clean.

My parents' bedroom door was always closed. It was the only room in our home that had a hardwood floor. It creaked and cracked if we ever tried to sneak out of bed and sneak into their room. Down the hall and past the bathroom was the room of my older sister, which was usually cluttered with small figurines and fantasy books and even some 1980s band posters. Off of the kitchen was a door leading down to the basement. We held tightly to the splintered railing as we went down into the cold cement area that housed a makeshift bar, dartboard, laundry facility, and a door that led to the garage. The garage door was always clustered with Boxelder bugs, cobwebs, and daddy longlegs, and walking across the cement floor that sloped into a drain always made my toes curl with anxiety. Though everybody probably has a basement that causes them to run quickly up the stairs at night when alone for the fear that something might grab your feet or be on your heels, this basement had more of a claustrophobic feel, as if maybe something would fall down on you and you'd never get out. You felt as if you were miles below the surface of the earth rather than just a level below, and the air always seemed heavy, dirty, and cold.

Our yard was always littered with blooming trees, the smell of lilacs was always ripe on the property line, and the bright green yard glowed at sundown when it was lit by the lightning bugs. The same lightning bugs that we would joyfully hunt and keep in Mason jars until they died. The garage my dad used as a workshop was his sanctuary, always cluttered with tools. While playing in the yard we would see him through the windows, welding, sparks flying through the air. At dusk the garage light would turn on, and the large, metal, chalky doors gathered bugs because of the huge light my dad kept going over our yard. It made for the perfect place to collect bugs, which I often pinned to Styrofoam (despite my mother's endless requests to leave them outside). My sister and I always ran barefoot, tended to the garden, and played with the animals all day long, and never truly felt as though the land had any presence of anger or violent entities. Yet we knew we were not alone.

The Native Americans who lived next door would bring us agate stones and arrowheads, and one time they even brought us our own dreamcatcher made from cat intestines. Everyone in the neighborhood was friendly, everyone knew everyone else's business, and our house was always bustling with people.

The Old Hag

I never gave the old woman a name, we just knew her as the old woman who used to live in our house. We knew she had died because the realtor told us she had refused assisted living for decades and her death was the only way her family could get her out of the house.

The lady I saw was hunched over, as if having some physical disability that kept her nose facing the floor, and her hair was always strung down her face by the force of gravity, covering the lines in her neck and jaw. The shadows created by her hair tussled over her head and draped over her shoulders seemed to hide the expression on her face; therefore, she always seemed a little mysterious. She moved slowly, cackled to herself quietly, and never made direct eye contact; it was as if she was in her own world and had no need to interact with anyone.

I usually saw her move across the living room when we were playing games on the carpet. I would build a fort behind the old rocking chair and gather my toys with me; just as I felt secure in my fort I would see movement outside the hallway. I would always expect that little movement from the corner of my eye to be nothing, and I would turn my head in surprise and see the old woman who so often joined our presence. She wore a long gown down to her ankles, old shoes that seemed so dirty they hardly stood out from the brown shag carpet in the living room, and she never made any sudden movements or loud noises. This old woman's ghost was a weekly occurrence, but never in all of my memories of her do I have anything that lingers as particularly scary, and there's nothing that I would say is even close to "demonic."

I'm not sure if she died in the home or had some traumatic story that gave her reason to stay in our home beyond her passing, but she was welcome and so she stayed. Some who research the paranormal and investigate strange phenomenon would suggest that because we gave her attention she lingered around for comfort. This theory suggests that if we had turned a blind eye, perhaps she would have left her house and continued on. Regardless, we gave her respect. It also comes to my attention that if this old woman didn't have some traumatic tale of violence and abuse, and nothing quite stood out as acute as someone being hung on the front yard oak tree, and of course I don't subscribe to the belief that our quaint home was ever a vortex to another realm; why then did we have so much paranormal phenomenon?

Why the Hauntings?

In all my years of experience, I still don't have an answer for why something is haunted. My husband gave me a great analogy: He has never had a paranormal experience and therefore finds it terribly hard to believe in the existence of something in the paranormal; however, in his thirty-eight years he has also never seen a tornado, but knows that they exist. Videos, photos, firsthand accounts and, yes, even popular television shows sensationalize the tornadoes that blister down the Bible belt each year and therefore they seem valid. Much of the same evidence can be found in the spiritual and paranormal community, and yet such disbelief and hokum is accepted. Many people go their whole life without ever being in or witnessing a tornado in person, and yet we know they wipe out towns and suck people up into their funnel in the sky quite often. I think this serves as a great analogy to those who have yet to have or may never have a paranormal experience; they do exist, and I can tell you that for sure.

Some people have a paranormal experience that is rather exciting and full of adrenaline and is a one-time happenstance that gives them a great story to tell for life. Others, much like me, my sister, and others in my family seem to have countless happenings, and I'm not naïve enough to believe that the haunting will ever end. Do I believe there is something wrong with me? Do I subscribe to the Christian belief that maybe I meddled once and now will forever pay the price on the physical realm to be haunted by those beyond the veil? Quite honestly, I don't presume to know an answer. I simply know what I can tell you, and what happened to me. I know, even with my experience of moving cups, slamming doors, creeks and bangs in the night, and voices in the dark, that these are not always spiritual entities.

Believe it or not, I am a skeptic who often finds rational everyday explanations for the bumps in the night, whether it pertains to Gestalt psychology (how our brain organizes information) or leaky faucets. For those experiences that cannot be explained, I am open to the spiritual possibility, but I don't ever jump to the conclusion that something is demonic, angelic, or even something of another dimension stepping through a portal to do me harm. I am aware that there is much to be learned, and I hope to be open to all those possibilities when the answers present themselves.

I help clients like I tend to help myself, by using education and experience to find ways to deal with the anxiety paranormal occurrences can bring into life. I teach clients ways to relax, meditate, remove the fear response, and even consider communicating with whatever it is that seeks your interaction and attention.

Eventually, when you learn to control your fear response and physical reaction, you can logically begin to separate the difference between what feels negative and what feels positive. You gain access and strengthen your own personal intuition.

I myself have found my intuition to be a great shield of protection, precursor to avoid harm, and deterrent of negative energy as well as something to help capture my attention so that I don't miss some of the most awe-inspiring epiphanies that my life has provided me thus far. I believe in the duality of nature and that this duality extends beyond the veil. I don't know if the old woman who haunted our home found comfort in us including her, but I know that by including her she has given me a great comfort in the paranormal; we are not alone.

One interesting note to mention before I move on to the darker tales of my past is that our home was remodeled when my parents got a divorce in the mid-1990s. All of the amazing paranormal activity, from cabinets moving, doors slamming, voices speaking, and reflections looking back at me in the mirror, ceased to exist for a few years after the home was demolished. A new house was built upon the foundation, and many changes in the family occurred. My father remarried, my sister moved out and went to college, and I grew into my teenage years in this newly remodeled home. I remember my stepmother hanging photos and old pictures on the wall, and after they had been hung I felt that the old woman didn't like them much. I often remember feeling her presence, but I didn't see her visually as I used to as a young girl.

There were a few nights sitting on the couch, watching television late into the wee hours, that I thought I saw her walk past the front windows out on our porch, but when I got up to see if she was there, it was nothing. I often awoke in the night, hearing something walking around in the brand-new attic that was full of insulation, and even when I told my dad of the noises he brushed it off as a possible animal and nothing to be worried about. Eventually, even the small sightings of the old woman and the feeling of her presence near me seemed to descend with the memories of my childhood and that old haunted house.

Yet, nearly a decade after moving out, I received a call from my stepmother. She knew I wouldn't think she was crazy because of the work I do in the paranormal, and told me she had started to see a woman looking at her from the front porch through the window.

She said the old woman had her hair pulled back up upon her head, and wore very old clothing. She described this old woman as just meandering about and, through the phone, after listening to my stepmother's experiences with the old woman, I grinned to myself. I assured my stepmom I did not think she was crazy; while the old woman's hair might have been slightly different, I knew that she had been in that house for many many years. It was then my stepmom confided in me that she not only saw the old woman walking past the front windows at night but that she also had seen other people in the home.

From this point on I knew our haunted house wasn't spiritually active because of the presence of my mother, sister, or me uniquely and/or because of our sharp intuitions. Instead, I knew that something indeed was special about that spot in Parkville, Missouri. It clearly didn't reside in the structure of the home, or the people who lived there, but nonetheless seemed to be a gathering spot for spirits.

I helped to ease my stepmom's anxiety and the validation of her witness to the old woman, and I finally found an old piece of my childhood that gave me sanctuary in the paranormal.

Now when I go home to my parents' house in Kansas City and stay in the upstairs guest room, I smile when I hear the creeks and cracks of the home. I say hi to the old lady when I come in and when I go, and I always double-check over my shoulder when I see something out of the corner of my eye.

TWO

The Ouija Board

I don't think my sister would be offended to read that she was often alienated as a child. Not just from our family who always seemed to be busy doing their own thing, but also by her peers and those in her social group. She was a loner and an introvert and always had her nose buried in a science-fiction book. Our mother was a fiery woman who often threw us under the bus and put us on the spot in public, creating the craziest of comedic parental scenes for which children get made fun of for years. Showing up drunk to school events, asking childhood boyfriends about their sex lives, and hitting on my friends' dads.

Our father was a hard-working man who, when he was home, was found tinkering away in his garage. He would get home from work, shower and change, and quickly find something to be busy doing for the rest of the night, either delving into the restoration of an old car or drowning out the busyness of life by mowing our two-acre yard.

My sister found refuge in her fantasy novels, books, and movies, and by using her grand imagination that never seemed to know any bounds. She was writing full-length books by the time she was ten, and hit puberty far before any of her classmates. My sister was smart and quiet, and hid behind thick glasses and chunky-cut bangs of dark hair that hung over her face. She was also quite intuitive.

We talked openly to the spirits in the home and the ghosts in our house and also exercised our imaginations all day every day. My sister even had an imaginary friend named "Boy," who for quite some time had his own spot at the dinner table. By the time I could recall having solid childhood memories, perhaps the age of five or six, my sister was in the beginning of her tumultuous teenage years. She had found a handful of cohorts, sprightly young teenagers full of muster and rebellious energy, to join her in her spiritual endeavors. They cast spells, created haunted houses for me and my friends to walk through, and let us stay up late at night with them while they babysat and we watched horror movies I was far too young to be watching. My sister and I had rabbit-feet key chains tied to our belts, and always threw a little salt over our shoulders. We knew how to use the lunar phases for gardening and affirmations and could recite scripture and prayer if needed. We brought lilacs into the home to please the spirits, made sure dreamcatchers were over our bed, and even put a bay leaf or two under our pillows for good dreams. We were, of course, off the beaten path.

It seemed that when we were too young to have friends over but old enough to have established childhood memories, mother was teaching us how to profile and read playing cards for telling futures. She was always teaching us unique ways to be the life of the party, and she stated that the more tools you had on your tool belt of life to get by, the easier things would be. Learning divination was one of those tools. I suppose everyone has superstitions and traditions in their family, but that seems to be all my family had in regard to my positive recollection. There were some pretty hard times growing up, but my fondest memories are learning how to use divination and spirituality to have faith and hope of something better around the corner.

We collected buckeyes, learned if romantic endeavors were true love by the juice of the bleeding heart plant, and even predicted the winter weather by the camouflage of the fuzzy woolly worm that crept through the fall season. Our mother was always very generous with her knowledge of superstitions and herbal remedies, and the naturalistic lifestyle seemed to blend into who we were as a family. We learned that the lunar cycles affected the garden and also our dreams, and we understood the phases of the moon for the goals of any prayers or spells. What some might consider a potion, my mother laughed, was another woman's lotion; she was always concocting mixtures for wrinkle-free creams and party elixirs.

Another gift from my late mother was her validation that spirituality was everywhere, and for some that meant a heavy devotion to their religious faith. When she would drop us off with our paternal grandparents, she knew we would be doing nothing but playing music, baking cookies, and reading the

Bible. She helped to explain bibliomancy and how to find great guidance and wisdom in any particular book that spoke to us; she said for my grandparents, that was the Bible. I may not be a devout Christian today, but I turn to the Bible for random scripture and do believe it is meant for me; coincidence and serendipity all fade away.

Spiritualism was also in reading tea leaves after we made our weekly pitcher of iced tea for the family. After brewing, adding the sugar, and leaving to stew in the sunlight so the tea didn't get cloudy, we would use the tea leaves to tell our fortunes.

I even remember mother explaining totem animals based on those animals that specifically spoke to us. I always loved the hippopotamus, the rhino, and the raven, and she told me stories similar to *Wind in the Willows* about characters with historical personal identities relating to the animal. After the whole whimsical tale, she would ask me if I then understood why that animal was in my life right now. I've since learned that form of divination also works in profiling.

When I was a teenager and learned that pendulums and electrical equipment were used as paranormal tools, it seemed humorous but it made sense. My mother and grandparents used to show us how to dowse with tree branches to help determine the best place to have a garden or plant a tree. If ever we were unsure of where to build our next fort, family members would encourage the use of Mother Nature and her wise guidance.

Turns out, this type of divination has been in human civilization for many hundreds of years. You can take a branch of a tree and gently but firmly hold it out in front of your body, then focus on a question. The branch will begin to move in the direction that is most truthful. Humans have dowsed for water, minerals in the soil, and, of course, we teenagers used it to find the best outfit to wear to the school dance. Divination, superstition, and the paranormal were so much a part of my life it's hard to determine when it ever started... it's just always been there. I guess that's why having a Ouija board story is surprising even to me.

Demons

I remember a childhood friend of mine always shaking her head against my request to play with the Ouija board. It was only so often I could steal it from my sister's room and keep it long enough for her not to notice and to share it with my own friends. Nonetheless, many of my friends had heard from their parents it was something that opened a gateway to a demon. Regardless of how much I detested and shared with them my own experiences, we usually ended up playing ghost in a graveyard outside in the backyard.

I suppose this is where I insert my own experience and opinion on what a demon really is. I may not be a devout Christian, but I do believe in Christianity's metaphorical interpretation of the universe and all the complexities in it. I do believe it is in our best interest to know that a higher consciousness is a God that has created us in its own image. I believe that we are His children and, in a way, we are all a Jesus Christ learning to forgive others and to make sacrifice. So many religions teach a simplistic faith to know that something is greater than yourself and to live for something, and die for something. For some, that something is vague and religion helps to fill in those pieces. For others, they prefer to remain whimsical and curious to the natures of the energy around us.

A demon is a religious entity said to be the personification of pure evil. The goal of the demon is to force a person to commit suicide and to relinquish the higher consciousness, the gift of life, and living with purpose. Because I believe in a higher good, from all the duality I have seen in nature, I know there must be an evil balance.

Evil is addictive, easy, impatient, unkind, and selfish. Evil can have a name such as one given to a demon in the biblical story, or it could be the spiritual sense of the seven sins. Perhaps your demon's name is Balthazar or perhaps your evil demon is gluttony. Evil can be a nasty thought you have in the back of your mind that refuses to leave. It can be the quick, harsh words spoken in anger to a loved one. I believe if you feed evil it will stay. Being the hard-working and devout Christian man my father was, he always recited the scripture that "the devil loves idle hands." I suppose that is why I have long since forgiven my dad for always being preoccupied and busy with something rather than doing nothing with me from time to time. I don't believe that evil finds us just because we're bored, but instead that it follows intent. I believe if you are self-loathing or have been surrounded by negative energy (stress and all of its many forms) you can fall victim to evil and, yes, even the metaphorical demonic possession.

In my life, I have fallen victim to many great evils and some of them have a name and some of them do not. Just as I believe evil lives and grows on intention, I also believe it can be dispelled with good intent. In the religious sense, this intention might be to seek out someone of strong will and education who has studied how to revoke a possession and who can use their belief in a higher God to enact a routine of exorcism to dispel the evil. If you believe through your Christianity that this is the best way to remove a demon, then I agree with you, it is.

Maybe you are more of a secular humanist or skeptic and simply know that you are plagued with some kind of a mental illness, curse, or dark rain cloud, and you have decided to make a change in your life to remove it, maybe you dispel your nameless demons with therapy, a new hobby, cleaning your home, or detaching from polluted friends. If you find this to be the best way to dispel evil in your life, I agree with you—it is.

I always saw that common seed as being belief and intent. I suppose that's why I am fearful and scared of what comes out of the abyss. I believe in something greater and good and by default I must therefore accept that there is a dark evil in this world. I have never intended to go out looking for them, but they have found me nonetheless. And I do believe the paranormal superstition that once you see them, they do indeed see you.

Chosen

Now of course being the little sister, I was the nemesis to my older sister and her friends. When they cultivated together in her room, giggling down the hall, they locked it shut tightly and made sure my fingers could barely fit under the door. I would press my ear to the hollow wood door frame and listen to them singing along to their music and telling scary ghost stories at night.

I remember one afternoon in particular that my sister's door creaked open and the curiosity reflected off the beam of light straying across the carpet. I knew it had been her mistake, but I was going to let it be my reward. I sat a few feet from the door; I brought my knees to my chest and my toes tightly under my bottom so that the light beam on the carpet didn't touch my shadow in the hall. I breathed quietly, and laughed under my breath as I spied on my sister and her friends. They were playing with that darn Ouija board.

Now my sister and I were raised on how to use divination. We did not see any divination tool different from another; we never thought that one tool could bring demons and one would hail angels. They are all used as a way to connect to a higher power and to seek guidance from something divine.

We had made our own Ouija boards in the past, but my sister had gotten the new one created by Warner and Warner and coveted this toy. I could hear her and her friends asking questions, getting their answers, and even using automatic writing to connect with the spirit they were talking to. Meanwhile, I didn't see anything in the hall, feel any great, dark presence loom past the door and into my sister's room, but I did seem to know even at that young age that they were making a connection with something.

Anticipation grew ... I wanted to be part of their circle. I wanted desperately to put my hand on that Oracle and feel the connection they had made. I wanted to be included in something cool, not just the casual interaction with the old lady in our house, but to something different. I couldn't take it anymore; I stood up and took a deep breath. I lunged into the door frame and opened up the door.

There I stood, waiting to get the greeting from my sister that I was in her domain and to get out, when instead I don't remember anything. I remember feeling the itchy shag carpet on my left cheekbone. I remember smelling the musty carpet against my nostrils and looking over to see the feet of my sister and her friends around me. I remember opening my eyes, becoming aware, and half-expecting that they would be shrieking in laughter to what was clearly my sister pushing me out of her bedroom successfully.

My sister never really pushed me ... or did she? I sat up and felt the hot and yet cool liquid run down my hairline and past my ear. I looked up at my sister and I did not see the face of an older sibling angry that I had stepped into her territory and who had broken up her party with her friends, but instead the wide-eyed face of concern. The ocular had flown from their hands, off of the Ouija board, more than five feet across the room, and hit me so hard in the forehead that it knocked me down and out into the hall. The ocular now sat halfway into the living room, buried within the thick carpet, and many feet away from my sister's door frame. Nothing had ever hit me before. Nothing that I could not explain had ever seemed to do me harm before, and at such a young age. Yet with already such a great amount of experience in this supernatural world, I was shocked.

I wish I could say something more presented itself, but a great part of me is glad that it didn't. We did not see a dark shadow person, feel stiff, cold bursts of air, or hear a dog growl coming from the refrigerator, but were simply left with a lot of questions. Nothing more came of the game-turned-headache.

Taboo

My sister still played the Ouija board with her friends time and time again after that experience, and eventually we wrote the event off. By the time I was eight years old, it seemed that the paranormal phenomena in our house became more active and, well, looking back, I attribute it to a few different things.

My mother was a very powerful psychic and also a very depressed addict. My mother had a great presence about her, and when it was good, it was amazing. However, when her energy was bad, it was very bad. I remember being fearful of my mother, a fear that, moment to moment, when she was in a bad mood we never quite knew what to expect. In retrospect, as an adult, I now know that she was dealing with some great mental illness, stress, and her addiction. For those who subscribe to the belief of a poltergeist, or the projection of chaotic energy, you can also understand that there were two young girls going through their adolescence in this home during the time of heightened paranormal activity. I think these factors had a big influence on the change from what was normal and casual spiritual action to turning to something a little darker. It could have been that my sister learned more about the darker sides of spirituality and that even some of her friends could have been practicing witchcraft, or it could have been due in part to the fact that we so actively gave these entities energy and attention. I will never know for sure, but I know I was fearful of the entities that seemed to be around my sister. It was the same entity that I believe showed itself that day, and drew blood from an eight-year-old girl just wanting to be included.

Many years later, after the house was rebuilt and my sister had moved out to go to college, I was in my own rebellious teenage stage. I had the self-prophetic feeling that I was something special, as most teenage girls typically do, and called on my spiritual experience quite often. My sister felt isolated and alienated by her intuition, whereas I kind of felt it made me unique and special. I loved to practice divination, to recite prayers and scripture in languages from Latin to French to English, and especially to be active in the paranormal research community within Kansas City.

When all of my girlfriends came over to my house one night with a Ouija board that they thought to be a spooky and tainted secret from their parents' adult den, I simply laughed. I got out all my books on the paranormal, got out a piece of paper to do some automatic writing like my sister and me and her friends had always done growing up, and I even drew a circle of salt and lit all of my candles and dimmed the lights for my friends.

I was desperately hoping my friends would have an experience that might give credibility to my many ghost stories, which I knew were real. Nearly an hour into our session, the ocular began to move. Who was moving it? Each person claimed not to be the one pushing, lifting fingers halfway through a given message that was nothing more than scrambled letters, and signs of growing desperation when no clear answers were ever given.

Just then, one of my friends sat back in the small three-sided, closed-off sun seat area that we were sitting in. We each were sitting on a pillow with our backs to a wall and huddled around the Ouija board. We took our hands off the ocular and I sighed with disappointment, "What do you want to do now?" I asked.

As our hands lay to our sides, and our backs to the wall, the candles all flickered as if the central air had turned on. We heaved with excitement and then laughed. Then the ocular began to move on its own. I immediately felt my stomach turn to knots; I was so fearful it was that same entity that had hurt me nearly a decade before. Usually the Ouija boards or other forms of divination were things that could be controlled, but this time we all watched the ocular—nothing pushing or pulling it—moving inches across the lacquered board all on its own. Even with my experience in the paranormal, I sat in disbelief. I had seen things move on their own, but I had never seen an ocular spell out a word with such precision and without assistance. None of us blinked. I don't even think any of us breathed. Then the ocular stopped. It had spelled, "TABOO."

One of my girlfriends stood up and, with the board balancing on our knees, it fell over onto the carpet. The ocular lay still on the carpet and the candles were still lit, but my friend ran over to the lights and flipped them all on. She opened my bedroom door and, with no laughter in her eyes, left the upstairs area completely.

We all joined her on the porch swing outside. That word, "taboo," didn't specifically mean anything to us, and the movement of the ocular wasn't harmful. I reassured them that we had experienced something really awesome and were lucky nothing negative did happen. A few minutes later, as my friend got off of the porch swing, she winced in pain. She threw her hand back behind her and grasped onto the shirt tucked into her pants and lightly rubbed her lower back. She asked us if there was something crawling on her, but nothing was. All three of us untucked her shirt and lifted it up above her bra strap, as she was persistent something was on her back. We couldn't believe what we saw.

A deep gash ran from the top of her shoulder blades down under her bra strap to her lower back. It wasn't the cliché three long scratches, but it clearly looked as though something had been dropped down her back. She burst into tears and called her mom to come get her. My friends and I all agreed that our Ouija board experience was strange. I didn't want to assume that someone getting scratched and the ocular moving on its own was a negative entity, but looking back at how scared everyone was and what my intuition had told me—the gut-wrenching feeling in the pit of my stomach—maybe it was.

So the question is, do I use a Ouija board today? Do I think the Ouija board is a gateway for evil since the majority of my experiences are negative? I don't find the Ouija board to be the best divination tool for the simple fact that it relies on a handful of factors that can easily be polluted. The Ouija board suggests you use more than three people, but the more people included in the session the more room for human error—moving the ocular through nervousness, suggestive thought, or malicious intent to create an adrenaline rush and entertainment for all. Perhaps a participant isn't interested, and therefore fakes the answers or even introduces negative energy into the session.

Whether you believe it's a tool communicating with spirits or not, you can see how the reliance on a handful of people can be a very subjective and murky tool for investigating. Since I am typically validating experiences for clients I want to use tools that are more objective, scientific, and have less room for human error. However, I would use a Ouija board today if the opportunity arose with little-to-no concern. I say this because I believe every divination tool, a tool in which you use with the intention of communicating with spirits, can come in many forms. My digital voice recorder, my camera, even my vocal cords can in some way be interpreted as the manipulation or use of a tool in hopes to communicate with the spirit. For this reason, I don't consider the Ouija board to be more evil than any other tool.

I believe the Ouija board has received a negative reputation due in part to the fact it is associated through Hollywood with negative and flamboyant outcries of demon possession. Teen horror movies and paranormal documentaries utilize the Ouija board because it makes for a wonderful prop. It has beautiful and cryptic handwriting, everyone seems to be channeling on some telepathic level, and, of course, the lighting always looks really cool as everyone is hunched like witches over their boiling potion. It's not nearly as entertaining to watch someone with a digital voice recorder or Ganzfeld Helmet. I believe any and every tool used with the intention of communicating with spirits can have an outcome. I believe that outcome and experience will be entirely based upon intentions, and therefore every paranormal opportunity has the possibility to be safe and effective. Intention and belief create reality.

What Are Demons?

I do not subscribe to the belief that the Ouija board is an evil gateway to demons. I don't believe that any one tool used in divination is any more negative or positive than another. Just as a Catholic might use metals and candles, or voodoo priestesses might use powders and teas, or a Pagan might use tinctures and flowers and the moon phases—they are all ways we communicate with the divine. Etching letters into a board and asking some entity to answer a question is all, in my opinion, quite innocent.

I believe it is the intentions of the person using the tool that depict the overall experience one will have. I also believe that the power created by someone who interprets, compared to the power created by someone who channels, are quite different from one another. It is one thing to cast runes, read tarot cards, or interpret tea leaves, and quite another to ask the spirit to do a walk-in and speak through you. I believe if you are someone who is not grounded, firm in some sort of faith, and well protected by a strong mental foundation, then asking another entity to share your physical body can be dangerous.

It is for this reason that I believe the Ouija board has a negative connotation; you are using your body to channel, in some way, shape, or form, through pushing the ocular. These forms of divination, even automatic writing, need to be done with a mindful awareness of the possible consequences, and therefore with someone who's comfortable taking any precautions necessary for what the worst-case scenario might be. Because I know and believe in an afterlife, and also know there are many questions and mystery around that realm, simply being prepared and mindful is all we can do.

Am I fearful of the Ouija board? No. Am I fearful of what might come through to communicate with me? Of course.

THREE

Beneath the Covers

A lot of clients and people who join me at paranormal lectures ask where the scariest places I have been to are and if I have ever experienced a dark entity. The truth is, I've experienced a lot of strange phenomena, but I'm still not quite sure if there was anything demonic or dark, or if it was simply my fear response to the stimulus that made me feel so uneasy. I try to explain to people that I can count on one hand how many times I've felt truly scared, scared to the point I knew I just had to get out, and the "or else" wasn't something I even wanted to imagine.

Lots of times things have jumped out at me, called my name in the dark, grabbed me from behind and startled me, and, yes, these experiences were scary, but I don't think that they're dark or evil. We have all had friends or family jump out and scare us, we've paid money to go to a haunted house to be frightened, and even taken the deep plunge down a huge roller coaster to experience the fear response our central nervous system gives when surprised or shocked; we don't consider these experiences evil. I guess this is the reason why I really do have such a small selection of what I would pull to when thinking of what has truly been dark.

As a psychologist, I think about suggestive thoughts quite a bit. How many people have watched a television show about ghost hunting and associate cold spots, low growls, dark shadow figures, and mysterious happenings in the night with something dark and evil? In my experience, I would say it's the majority. I find it interesting, when you consider the electromagnetic spectrum, that the duality finds positive or angelic experiences to be warm, high-pitched noises and associated with bright lights; like there is this polar opposite to good and evil and it's illustrated by how they manifest. When I think back to the very first experience I ever had with something that scared me, really and truly scared me, what was I also experiencing? Well, the memory that comes to mind is one that I have yet to replicate in my work experience or in all of my paranormal adventures; it is unique. I know with all of my heart that it was not my imagination and I can recall it perfectly well even now, almost thirty years later.

From the Darkness They Came

We did not have air conditioning in that small haunted house I grew up in. Even though the summers got quite warm in Missouri, windows would be open and a cool breeze usually helped lull us to sleep at night. The cool air snuck in my window, the crickets were chirping out on the lawn, and the low hum of the garage light buzzed in the room. My Little Mermaid curtains hung from the top of the window to the bottom of my carpet and blew in the wind, and just beyond the window screen I could see our backyard cluttered with thick oak trees; I could even see the stars.

There were lots of animal noises outside, noises creaking from within the old home, and of course those mysterious happenings that occurred quite frequently into the night, and yet I always got to sleep just fine. As a young girl I was quite frequently victim to night terrors, but as the doctor suggested to my parents, I would simply work through the night terrors and my parents were encouraged to never wake me up. The night terrors kept me kicking, talking, screaming, and turning in bed most all nights for hours. Though my mind was active, I never remembered what had happened the night before in my dreams. Some mornings I had bumps and bruises from falling out of bed or flailing around, but I never really did recall what was giving me the night terrors. The content must still lie somewhere deep in my subconscious. That particular night, however, I did have trouble getting to sleep, and I remember every dragging detail to this day.

A fly was keeping me awake. I was around seven years old and quite aware of my bedroom (which was the same way it had been since my parents removed the crib). I'd always faced the same window and said good night to the same moon. The covers were etched tightly around my armpits from where my dad had tucked me in, a tight "Sarah-Burrito," and my glow-in-the-dark dinosaur (an Ankleosaurus, my favorite) sat upon my chest of drawers by the closet. My bedroom door creaked open and I could see that the door to my parents' bedroom was closed and latched across the hall. The house was dark at night, and my sister had closed her bedroom so the hallway was a pitch-black dark opening in the corner of my bedroom just feet from the foot of my bed. I watched the moon; I listened to the animals, and kept insistently blowing at the housefly that would land on my nose. He buzzed back and forth across my face and it was his annoying presence that reminded me I was far from falling asleep. His wings twitched and it tickled my skin. Then I saw something out of the corner of my eye…

As usual, many things happened in our haunted house, so I didn't feel scared but simply looked into the hallway. I blinked; I stared long and hard, and kept blowing at the housefly on my nose. Nothing was there. I said good night to what might be lingering in the hallway and went back to trying to find my way to sleep. I shifted beneath the covers and blankets and repositioned myself in the center of the bed with my stuffed animals close by. I kept watching the curtains blowing in the wind, while I blew spit at the housefly still hassling around my face, and glanced from time to time into the hallway; just being awake.

Movement. I saw it move again, only this time I felt very unsafe. I felt as though something was watching me from every angle in my room. The small room seemed to be shrinking and the sudden silence of an open room grew stuffy with a claustrophobic presence in the air. I didn't feel paranoid about something in one particular corner or even the dark hallway that had started to take my attention, but instead I felt unsafe in my own skin. I had never felt this scared before. It…they, could see me. I was alone, in my private bedroom and just about to fall asleep when they came from out of the darkness.

The Wow Wow Wibble
Woggle Wazzie Woodle Woo!

Usually as a child, when something scares you, you run to your parents. You cry, search for their embrace, and find the comfort of their arms; it makes everything better. The interesting thing about whatever it was that was now in my room and watching me was that I was so overwhelmingly terrified, I was too afraid to make a sound and far too scared to run to the sanctuary of my parents' room beyond the doorway. The fly had landed on my nose but it didn't tickle, it reminded me that I was awake and I wasn't dreaming. I couldn't swat him away and his sticky legs pranced over my perspiring brow. I could hear my blood flowing, I could hear my breath getting quicker, and I was trying to talk myself into relaxation so that I wouldn't make a sound. Maybe if I didn't move, didn't make a sound, whatever it was would go away.

The pressure in the room got stronger and it felt more difficult to breathe, even though the curtains were still blowing in the breeze. I truly didn't understand! I didn't see anything in the room, nothing at all. The old woman wasn't coming in to check on me, nothing was screaming in the darkness, and yet, despite no ghoulish figure, the presence was undoubtedly "there." Then the blackness in the hallway somehow managed to get darker. There was no shape taking form, no man stepping out from the shadows as a dark, evil figure, but the hallway seemed to become so pitch-black that even the shadows in the room were gray in comparison. I almost felt as though I would be sucked into the hallway if I were to get out of bed and run across the hall to my parents. It was like a black hole, a vacuum, a mesmerizing darkness. I didn't move. I didn't breathe. I lay still as I could, just waiting for this to pass or for me to fall asleep. I repeated in my mind, "It's fine, it's not real. It's fine, it's not real…" My stomach tightened, I could feel the sweat on my brow starting to drip, and the housefly still crawling up over my furrowed forehead. I was mesmerized by the darkness in the hallway, so much so, I felt my eyes becoming dry because I was too fearful to blink.

Then I saw something. I hoped it was light beaming from the living room at the end of the hallway, or even my sister opening her door perhaps having intuition to come save me. I focused as hard as I could on this new image taking form in the middle of the dark hallway. In the center of the door frame, floating all on its own. Something was coming toward me, but it was only a few inches tall. I was still too scared to move, but I stared, watching this new movement with anticipation. The small figure coming forth from the dark hallway was getting bigger, almost as if the hallway that I knew was only a few feet long actually extended miles into the darkness; like an illusion stretching beyond the horizon.

As the figure got larger, marching in a strange rhythmic pace toward my bedroom door out of the darkness, another figure appeared behind it. One after the other, it seemed a gaggle of beasts were walking out of the hallway down some long corridor into my bedroom; from the darkness from which they came... conjuring near my bedside.

I wanted to scream. I wanted to move, but I just lay there. I had never seen anything like these creatures before. If I had to describe their appearance, it would be something similar to a creation out of a Jim Henson muppet movie... very inhuman and beast-like, but very self-aware and ominous. Just as the creatures in their rhythmic pace began to approach my bedroom door, I found the energy to pull the covers over my head. Quickly darting beneath. In a quick burst of courage, I lunged under my cotton sheets and clenched my hands tightly over my ears. However long I had stared into the darkness to watch these creatures come toward me, I had been unable to move. It was out of desperation that I found it within me to lay still under the covers. I didn't hear anything, but I still felt as though I was being watched.

Stealing My Breath

The housefly I had wished dead over and over all night long joined me under the covers, and together we breathed slowly and quietly for what seemed like forever. The fly was my companion in this nightmare. I didn't dare peek out from underneath the covers; the curiosity of a seven-year-old was no match for the terror I was experiencing. My intuition gripped far beyond my imagination and told me to just be still. I began to struggle with my breath. The thick covers did a wonderful job blocking out any images of a beast looming in my bedroom, but also blocked out the fresh air. I could feel my blood pumping beneath my skin, and my forced breath was becoming loud and wet; I needed to just trust that those creatures weren't in my bedroom.

I waited until I didn't have any more air under the sanctuary of my covers and closed my eyes as tightly as I could. I swallowed, hearing the dry spitball falling in my throat. I clenched the covers, and with my white and coiled fingers, and with my eyes closed, I threw back the bed sheets to gasp for fresh air. Suddenly the cool breeze I was looking forward to felt cold and wet on my neck. I forced my eyes open... and again was struck with fear.

I had taken a deep breath with the creature just beyond my lips. I had never seen and never want to again see this snarling jowl. It was just inches from my mouth, panting. It had been standing there, gawking at my body lying still beneath the covers this whole time; it had been stalking inches outside the cotton tent.

Tears welded into my eyes and though I wanted to close my mouth I didn't want to move either. There must have been eleven or twelve of them, none of them looked the same, and they were all strange, ghoulish things standing above my bed. They were touching me; they weren't covered in blood and didn't appear as gory images from some horror movie, but instead were heaving at my bedside. Like an old person hunched over in laughter so deep that they made no noise, these things had their mouths open and were heaving in rhythmic nature. I stared at the one closest to me, just inches from my face, and felt lost. I had been terrified for so long during this experience that I just felt weak and hopeless. I finally rolled my head over to the side of my pillow as if to just surrender, I couldn't lay still in fear any longer.

At that moment they were gone.

It was my bedroom again. Just me and the fly. I looked back down into the hallway and I could see details of the carpet against the shadows; it wasn't just darkness anymore. I felt my wet hair, my neck, caressed my arms to make sure I was all accounted for. There was texture in the shadows once more, there was a breeze in the room, and though I felt the lingering emotions of fear I felt like ... myself. I rolled over, and forced myself to sleep.

Was It All a Dream?

Ever since I was a young child I've always had very vivid dreams. I've had a mild obsession with dream interpretation and it was a daily routine that over our bacon and cereal each morning we would share our nightly adventures. Some of my dreams were used in childhood stories that I wrote in school and others were more haunting. I honestly believe that because we talked about them, gave them importance, and looked forward to having more each night, my sister and I have always been very vivid dreamers.

To this day, I have a belief that there are three types of dreams: a symbolic dream, a precognitive dream, and a cathartic dream.

A symbolic dream is how your own subconscious brain delivers and deciphers its trials and tribulations through the night's rest. Just as a computer defrags and updates software, your brain is connecting all the dots without any outside stress and throwing bits and pieces to your consciousness for the waking hours. I believe this language of the subconscious mind is very cryptic and therefore completely individualized and subjective to the dreamer. If you're asking me to interpret your dreams, I'm going to quiz you and walk you through talk therapy on your interpretations of the symbols you see.

A precognitive dream can be associated with astral travel or even remote viewing, because one does have the sense that they are aware. Your physical body might be sleeping, but you are omnipotent and you are present; you are mindful, and you can almost make decisions that project the outcome of the dream. Usually this is what happens with the experience of déjà vu; you had a precognitive dream at one time that you would get to this point and you have arrived. Take note. Precognitive dreams can be the vision of a warning, a connection to a world event, or a projection of future stressors you're trying to deal with and plan for.

A cathartic dream is a simple emotional release that is required of the brain to function. A cathartic dream runs parallel with the rapid eye movement cycle and isn't necessarily anything meaningful other than the undercurrent of the brain while it rests. Just as we might take a break from a chaotic moment to go outside and scream, our brain just needs to let things go. Sometimes we remember a bit of the catharsis as a very strange and irrational dream.

When I consider this theory of dreams, I look back on the creatures that came to me from the hallway. I know I wasn't dreaming. These huge, hairy, hovering monsters from the dark snarled at my bedside that night and then retreated back into the shadows. I remember their dry skin. I remember their wet eyes. I remember the damp and musty smell of an old basement and rotting flesh searing my nostrils as I tried to avoid their warm breath on my face. I have never seen anything like those monsters since; but I have not forgotten. As I said before, I experienced night terrors as a child and still do as an adult, but I don't suffer from any other sleep disorders. I don't have sleep apnea, I do not suffer from sleep paralysis, and I don't have any neuropathy of any of my limbs.

In the field of transpersonal psychology, it is reported that one out of every three people suffers from some type of sleep disorder. I know mine well, and it is night terrors. That night in my bedroom, when I saw the dozen or more creatures, I wasn't struck with a sleep disorder; the tightness in my chest was from fear. It wasn't that I couldn't move my limbs, because I remember the burn in my muscles as I tried to lay still under the covers, praying I *wouldn't* move a muscle. It's true I had tightness of breath, but it was because I didn't want any more of the evil beings inside of me by breathing in their smells. I wanted them completely gone. I was aware, and I was scared to death.

Though neither my parents nor my sister ever experienced anything quite like my hallway monsters, as I sometimes called them, we were all in agreement that something
definitely haunted our little house. It wasn't until I was in my
mid-twenties that a friend of my sister's had read a status
on one of my social networking sites about my childhood
home. She sent me a private message chiming in about how
terrified she always was to stay over, because if she had to go
to the bathroom in the middle the night that meant going
down the hallway between the bedrooms. When I asked
her why she was so fearful of the hallway, she said she had
always seen monsters in the shadows.

It does always seem to be the abyss, the shadows, those
dark places that causes fear. In the field of psychology, I have
to wonder if it's some projection of a nightmare deep within
the psyche or whether it's the duality of Mother Nature; the
opposite of the light is the dark. Regardless, the abyss has
always been a curious and dark place I tend to wander ... Not
just at night.

FOUR

A Reoccurring Dream

It is funny how much the paranormal, psychology, and parapsychology are all wrapped into my life. The paranormal was a part of my childhood experiences that led to a fascinating hobby that later turned into a career. When I worked with clients as a hypnotherapist while also doing parapsychological research, I came into contact with conspiracy theories, ghosts, what some believe to be demonic entities or poltergeists, and even alien abduction.

Not everyone considers alien abduction or an alien experience to be paranormal, I suppose it is still somewhat paranormal because it remains an invalidated experience of fear. Alien abductions definitely share the taboo that those with a paranormal occurrence experience, and also share lasting psychological effects and anxiety. Those who have a paranormal experience are fighting skepticism to validate what they believe has occurred to them, just as those with an alien abduction encounter are trying to do. It would seem the majority of people want to believe and find that the coincidence and statistics leave the option open-ended as to whether we are alone on this planet. Spiritually speaking, both the paranormal and alien abduction share many similar qualities. I didn't always put the two together so closely until I began my work as a hypnotherapist.

I began to do some of my own soul searching and was working with some amazing neuropsychologists and hypnotherapists when I found dream interpretation and recall to be important tools for me. I began to dissect what fears I had outside of those biologically instilled within us as a species, and where the fears came from. It all came back to a reoccurring dream and an interesting experience I had growing up as a small girl in our haunted home.

The Dream

I couldn't have been more than two or three the first time I experienced this dream. I know this because I vividly remember trying to get out of my crib when feeling the anxiety of the dream after waking; seeing the spindles and the drop below to the carpet. During all of my regressions, I've told of the experience and how terrified I was waking up (even at such a young age) and escaping my crib to go find my parents. I could see my little fingers wrapped around the wooden spindles and I could feel myself hoisting up over the sidebar. My body collapsed underneath my arms

as I fell to the carpet below and I quickly ran to my parents
(not daring to look over my shoulder at the window in my
bedroom behind me). Because this was the first time I had
experienced the dream, recalling all of the details was difficult, but I was familiar with the terror associated with my
response. It was a fear I knew well.

A few years later, at the age of five, I felt that same terror again as I awoke in my sleep. I wasn't sure if I was awake
or not (almost as if a lucid dreamer knows that they're not
completely in the physical but they're consciously aware of
their decisions and their actions). I looked out the window
that faces our backyard and saw something approaching.

My eyes grew dry as I stared deep beyond the opaque glass
dusted with greasy fingertips and the crusty residue left behind
from years past. Gaining a good focus was difficult. But slowly
I allowed my peripheral vision to seep in and I could begin
to see the outline of something against the clouds outside.
Smaller, small, bigger, bigger ... Close. It was this creature very
much like a pterodactyl flying through the sky and toward my
bedroom window; it was as if my curious gaze had made contact with the creature and it was locked into my tractor beam
of mesmerizing terror. My window was open and there was
no screen, just my curtains blowing between myself and the
outdoors and I knew this pterodactyl was going to enter, that it
was going to come and hurt me somehow.

When it landed in the backyard with a quiet thud, I simply
saw fire behind it as it tried to stick its head in the window to
grab me. The stretched skull couldn't fit inside the windowsill

and past the boundaries of the wall, but it kept banging its face against the house to try to poke its beak through and into my room. I could smell the odor of the creature; I could feel a coldness coming from its presence, and I could see that its skin was smooth and wet. At that age I was quite obsessed with dinosaurs, and though it appeared to be like one I had seen in one of my many books, the identity of the creature was misplaced. It looked like a dinosaur, but I knew that it wasn't. I didn't know what it was.

Déjà Vu

I ran from my room as fast as I could, slipping on the way out and looking down at my hands on the carpet...suddenly having déjà vu of the same moment a few years before when I had fallen from my crib. I had been here, running from this creature, escaping for my life, and seeking the sanctuary of my parents in the late hours of the night. It was happening again. The carpet felt the same under my toes and my breath was just as rapid as I got up to run and meet my parents, who were in the basement rec room. After the shock dissipated that this was something that wanted me and wasn't a random happening of a paranormal occurrence, a paranoia seeped in. How long was I going to have to keep running before I faced this thing? How many times would it come back for me? I ran through the living room and felt my feet stick to the tile floor in the kitchen as I rounded the door to the basement. My soggy hands sweaty with fear clenched onto the dry wooden handlebar, and without thinking of splinters, without being nervous something would grab my heels through the back of the empty stairs, I ran swiftly to my parents. I remember going to them. And that's all I remember.

A Burning Ring of Fire

At the age of nine or ten, somewhat versed in the paranormal and having an open dialogue with my parents about any strange happenings in the house, the dream happened again. This time when I awoke I knew the creature had already been in my room and had already taken me somewhere and that I was just returned to my bed. My body was coming out of shock at the fact I wasn't sleeping in my bed but standing at my window looking out at the backyard. This time I didn't see a strange pterodactyl creature, but I did see a circle of fire just in front of our shed about five hundred yards away from where I stood. I didn't see a craft, I didn't see a creature, but my body felt different.

The next morning I remember hearing my sister talk about my dad discovering something strange in the backyard. He had been out tending to the lawn when strange markings were found burnt into the ground just in front of our shed out back. My sister laughed at the possibility maybe we had aliens and even her talking about the possibility overwhelmed my body and mind with a paranoia and fear. It was as if I knew even talking about it or thinking about them would bring back their presence to check on me. Coincidence or not, shortly after this experience I started my menstrual cycle at the early age of just nine. I was already showing signs of endometriosis and I felt a level of shame within me I had never had before that moment.

I had the dream every few years, each time seeing fire in the backyard and knowing some inhuman creature was visiting me, but I never saw a face and I never felt as though I was onboard a craft. My experience was different than most of those with whom I work and didn't have some of the same cliché themes. My experiences weren't adorned with cold, sterile operating rooms decorated with sharp objects, and they usually did not include me being lifeless on a table staring up at slender figures with big bulging black eyes. I did, however, have similar symptoms, both dissociative and psychic, in and around this occurrence. Even in my hypnotherapy sessions, my mind would still not allow me to uncover all the details of the dream. I know that I will have it again soon and I'm always fearful of the night it will return to me. However, I am thankful that the experience gives me an amount of empathy needed to work with those sharing the same experience, and the anxiety related to a strange happening.

In regard to alien abduction, there always seems to be a sex-related theme of fertilization issues, molestation, and an overwhelming sense of shame. Women who often find themselves infertile, due in part to ovarian issues, ironically have an empathetic response to alien abductions, or have their own firsthand experience. As someone who is well-versed in psychoanalysis and dream interpretation, even though most of the details are still repressed, the reoccurring themes are intriguing.

FIVE

The House for Sale

Being someone who travels the country and talks with people around the world about their paranormal experiences means that I get a lot of questions about my own experiences, especially in regard to shadow people. A shadow person is both a supernatural and metaphorical concept of visions of a tall, dark, humanlike figure in silhouette. These shadow people, partly because they never have any detail or defined characteristics, are typically thought to be male, and therefore are also coined as gray men or shadow men.

I am not sure whether it is modern television entertainment that has glorified the shadow person or dark entities, but it seems to be a preoccupation to those interested in the paranormal. Depending on whether you find yourself a skeptic, a spiritual paranormal researcher, or someone who is unsure of this phenomenon, there is a history and link to modern folklore, as well as the reoccurring theme we see in popular culture today. Many within the paranormal field believe that a dark shadow person is that of a negative entity. I will say that it is perhaps an interesting correlation to the electromagnetic spectrum that dark energies, shadow people, low growls, and deep voices seem to accompany cold spots, and all of these are on one end of the electromagnetic spectrum.

The opposite polar end of the electromagnetic spectrum suggests a unique duality. Angels, positive entities, and high-pitched singing or children's voices are associated with a warm and bright light. Regardless of this subconscious duality of association that we see in the Yin and Yang, history has a number of legends and belief systems that illustrate the presence of these dark, shadowy figures; whatever they might be.

Working in the field of psychology, I always have to remain somewhat skeptical to the possibility that seeing a dark shadow figure, whether it is in peripheral vision or in direct contact, could be associated to a psychological condition. Some severe psychological mental illness or neurological conditions, even adverse side effects in too many common medications, can cause illusions, hallucinations, and distorted visual impairments. Even the ever-so-common sleep deprivation can cause someone to see things that may not be physically present. With all of the many possibilities and explanations aside, the shadow people or dark apparitions that haunt so many folklores and urban legends is something I have experienced in my life. Keep in mind, according to witness testimony I have been to some of the world's most terrifying places, from sanatoriums to the catacombs of France, but it was an old house that has remained one of the scariest of my experiences.

I believe I was around the age of eleven. I was spending the afternoon with a friend with whom I often was dropped off when my parents had to work. It was a hot summer day and the sun was shining brightly. My friend's aunt had pulled up in the driveway and excitedly burst from her car, explaining that she had just bought her dream home and wanted us all to come see it. My girlfriend and I bounced into the backseat, clicked our safety belts on, and happily rode along in the back of her aunt's car probably twenty miles outside of town. We pulled up to a beautiful three-acre home in the outskirts of a Missouri town. The whole yard was well-kept and decorated with large oak trees. As we parked under the shadowy trees we could see the house peeking out over the end of the drive. The house was an aging Victorian home with a large wooden wrap-around porch, adorned with a creaky swing. My girlfriend and I jumped from the car and asked if we could run through the house for which her aunt smiled and agreed. We darted across the lawn, up the stairs, and through the screen door, pushing our way past the unlocked entryway. The house had no furniture and every noise we made echoed through the first floor.

Just as most Victorian homes greet guests with a large wooden banister, this old house was no different. Wooden spindles decorated the staircase that easily went up three floors. We could run to the top and scream down to the bottom and sing songs that echoed through the entire house. We decided to play hide and seek.

As my friend tucked her head into the mud room entry, I quietly creaked up the staircase, going up and down a few times just to add confusion, and ended at the top floor. I walked down the hallway to the second door on my left and into a small bedroom that might have been the perfect nursery. It was a small room, with the sunshine reigning brightly across the wood floor and through the window that had an arched top and a sun seat. There were two closets in the bedroom, one on each side of the room. I chose the smaller closet in the corner and quickly laughed my way into the tight little spot, closing the door behind me. Immediately upon closing the door and hearing the doorknob click into place, my happy adrenaline turned to panic. Sunshine was not creeping under the door and the tight closet had become completely black. I tried to reach for the door handle but instead flung my arms above me, trying to grab onto the single string that hung from the light bulb on the ceiling. I remember feeling my back pressed against the thin wood of the closet walls and I could feel my chest tighten as I struggled to breathe.

Finally my fingers felt the thread and wrapped quickly around to pull down the light. When the light turned on, all I could see were drawings and strange marks on the inside of the closet wall. These marks were there when I happily ran in just moments earlier. I almost felt as if I was outside of my body, and perhaps living a claustrophobic nightmare of someone who had been trapped in this closet many years before.

I started to scream. I knew that the house was empty and that someone would surely hear my calls for help, but time seemed to stand still. I turned the light back off and felt for the door and pushed my way back through into the happy, bright room I was once in just moments before. I backed away from the small closet, and despite the bright sunshine wrapping around me and warming my body, I felt cold. I had a feeling come over me that I was in an extremely large amount of danger and, though I knew I was alone, I felt the presence of someone else with me in the room. I backed slowly away from the closet, not even blinking, and as I found my way to the door of the small bedroom something began to walk out toward me.

A large shadow figure of what appeared to be a broad-shouldered man leaning slightly to the left walked right toward me. He didn't have clearly defined legs or even arms, and was more of a silhouette. As it walked from the closet toward me in the hall the sunshine piercing through the window did not cause the entity to be opaque, and it was as if the figure consumed everything, even the light. I stood at the top of the staircase knowing that I wanted to turn and run as quickly as I could, but I couldn't even breathe nor could I take my eyes off this creature.

It did not have a face, it did not have eyes, but I knew it was looking right at me. Just as it stopped a few feet from my body its head tilted slowly to the left and then in an instant the horrible gut-wrenching fear in my body seemed to explode. I don't remember seeing the entity move or eject arms to push me, but I fell backward down the first flight of stairs. As I rolled and crawled my way down the remaining staircase to the front porch I looked back and did not see anything staring back in my direction. However, I was not willing to go back into the house to finish our game of hide and seek, and though normally a very rebellious and curious Sarah would go explore the closet one more time, everything in my being felt as though I was in harm's way going back into the house. I waited the rest of the afternoon in the car.

I have not seen a shadow person since. My experience didn't come with a gaping horrific story of the house that was a home to murder, and the experience was mine alone. Many years later the aunt came into a restaurant where I was waiting tables. I curiously asked her how she was doing in her house on the outskirts of town, and she lightly laughed that the home didn't last long. She suggested that things did not work out in that house and she took a job closer to the city, but she seemed to have a strange curiosity in her eye that I could empathize with. After all, who asks about a house more than a decade later when it was just a one-day adventure for everyone who came along that afternoon?

When I have clients describe to me the fear they experience with their shadow person encounter, I can empathize. I guess the closest thing I can associate it with is when you're a child ascending from the basement at night. You quickly hasten your steps and wonder if something might pull your ankles down below and you run faster and faster up the staircase, relieved when you make it to the top. Or the feeling that comes over you on a late, dark night when you walk to your car alone in an abandoned parking garage. When you reach for your keys as quickly as you can, look over your shoulder, and seem to believe somehow that there is someone out to get you. It's not something that can be rationally explained, though some would call it intuition, you just have a feeling that resembles the fight-or-flight of our central nervous system that takes over without logical thought. Everything in you feels a sense of fear and it cannot be something one completely understands until they have an experience of their own. Mine will always be that old Victorian house and the shadow person that came from the closet.

I have seen shadow people since this experience, but this dark entity stands out as a particularly negative experience, because I truly felt fear. It was a fear that stretched far beyond the realms of mortality. It was not just a fear for my life, but something even more supernatural. If something non-physical was defying all the laws as we believe them to be in nature, and clearly was violent and aggressive, to what ends did it have power over me? I suppose I have always assumed spiritual beings to be of a higher evolved authority to myself. Therefore, I have always revered spirits and entities with a great level of respect; they are on the Other Side. They do as they please, and sometimes maliciously so.

SIX

Coffey Road

I like to believe that every small to medium town in America has the spooky house on the corner, or even a strange story about a lookout point where a manly creature lurks about, leaving a bloody hook on a car door handle. Yarns are a large part of culture, folklore, superstition, and community; I think one of the most amazing things about human civilization is the fact that our community keeps scary tales. I've often tried to determine whether these stories are to teach a lesson, scare and deter children from some dangerous scenario, or if they just exist because we keep telling them; it's fun to be scared. Well, in the small community of Parkville, Missouri, there was a road on the edge of town my dad used to have scary stories about.

Every time we drove from the old store by the highway back to our house, we would swiftly drive past this overgrown gravel road branching out from the main stretch. The story changed from time to time, but the foundation of the scary events that took place down the road were consistent. My dad said there once was a glorious bed and breakfast down that road where old travelers used to stop.

Kansas City and its surrounding communities have always been a great stopping point for fur traders, those in the border wars, and especially those in the slave trade. A beautiful B&B just shy of the Missouri River and down the length of Coffey Road was said to always have open doors and a full table. One day, while travelers were bustling through the house playing cards on the porch, helping in the kitchen, or tending to the garden in the back, a rough gang of men stopped in for business. They gathered all of the guests and staff and locked them in rooms on the second floor. They asked everyone for their jewelry and valuables and then molested or raped the women of their choice. After taking all they could, the men locked the doors and burned the bed and breakfast; no survivors were reported. Now, I have never found the story in the newspaper, and it's not something to be memorialized each year despite its travesty. Instead, the story was one of "those tales."

I have not only heard the story from my dad, but other adults that I had been in the car with as we ventured past that road. I would always try to tackle some detail to ease my curiosity, and most of the time the adults took the bait. They would reiterate this horrible story that I had heard so many times before at the B&B at the end of Coffey Road. Unfortunately, we were always just driving past. I begged, I pleaded, I even bartered with my allowance for us to drive down the road; no one, however, took that bait.

Instead, I grew older and Coffey Road grew even more overgrown. Adults stopped trying to scare me with these tales and I stopped asking to hear them. The story of Coffey Road almost all but left my mind until one night I noticed a hesitation under the gas pedal when I myself was driving alone past the place known as Coffey Road. This hazy gravel road was now camouflaged into the tree line at an intersection. It wasn't a dusty stretch but instead a scuff in the well-paved highway buzzing around a now-crowded residential neighborhood. Unless you were looking, you would barely notice the turn at all as you sat waiting for the red light to turn green. But there I was, at a stall in the road as the light turned to green. There were no other cars out that late. I was completely alone. Despite my intuitions, I had unearthed a curiosity within me, one that had grown and barely died inside of me for all those years. But my mature rationality kept me from turning down Coffey Road. I went home.

It Lingered

The next day, when a class lecture had turned to talking in the back row, I asked some of my fellow students who lived near Coffey Road if they ever grew nervous of the old story. No one knew what I was talking about. I laughed off the embarrassment of my childhood obsession, thinking perhaps it *was* just a tale, when another student gawked over my shoulder and chimed in, "That is the same place my sister swore she saw some demon or something."

Something within my soul perked. I couldn't help but ask my classmate to tell me more. "What on earth do you mean?" I asked.

"She was out late, driving with her boyfriend, and drove down that old overgrown road. She thought the car might get stuck, but they just kept driving into the tree line and it went on for quite some time. Then she said her car began to act up and they looked up in the road ahead to see their headlights shining on some creature. She barely caught some of it on her camera phone, but it is kind of spooky. It's like some big black void that's hunched over and stares at you as it walks across the road."

Of course I had never heard tales of anything like this, but it did make me wonder if maybe a ghost appears differently to different people. Maybe there were evil robbers that still roamed the woods at night in that area. Maybe their evil deeds had condemned them to roam the earth. That weekend, I was sure to explain to my sister, who was home from college, that we had to go exploring down Coffey Road. Cat was always my partner in crime when exploring the unknown as a child. She was my sister, eight years older than me, and had lots of experience in the paranormal realms. Her then-boyfriend laughed, "I can't believe you both believe in all that stupid stuff." He proceeded to laugh and chuckle under his breath and slew out as many dumb jokes as he could about ghosts.

We had heard plenty of people say this when they came to stay at our house, and then, of course, run out the next morning with their lives changed forever. I think sometimes my sister and I liked to scare people with her paranormal experiences just because it stroked her ego and let us know we were strong women; we were survivors of some pretty crazy stuff.

"All it takes is one experience," I exclaimed. "One experience that leaves you wondering. And you will question everything for the rest of your life." Now, despite the opportunity to jump onto a paranormal soapbox, I honestly wanted nothing more than to just grab my sister and go investigate the end of Coffey Road. It had been waiting all these years after all. So I stepped back with my pride, my ego, off my soapbox. I smiled and he knew all his silly skeptical jokes did not annoy me.

We did the easiest thing to get a man to cooperate—we dared him to join us. We gathered our tape recorders, electromagnetic field readers, flashlights, and put on our hiking shoes.

My classmate was right, once you passed the tree line, the gravel road seemed to just get deeper into the forest. It was just wide enough that we could drive down the road without completely damaging the car, but not quite big enough if we had to turn around. Farther and farther, deeper and deeper, we drove the car to the very end of the property line. The car steadily grumbled over the gravel at a speed low enough to keep from kicking up more dust and making the visibility worse. However, we had to go fast enough to keep up a momentum. All of us had a pit in our stomachs; what if something did jump out? We weren't sure if this was where we began to hike in hopes of finding some collapsed building of an old B&B, but we figured it was a good place to start.

Cat's boyfriend insisted he would stay in the car and keep it running if we had to make a quick getaway. My sister and I both laughed at each other, wondering if he was truly trying to be practical or if he might really be scared something could reach out and grab him. We started walking into the forest.

Hellhound Growling

Just as the car and its bright headlights were dim over our shoulders, my sister and I both intuitively stopped in our tracks. We were nearly six hundred feet from the car, and despite the continued hike ahead of us, we both began to feel a little uneasy. Something wasn't right. We looked at each other, and listened as if to determine that perhaps our fear was triggered by some animal in the forest. It did feel as though we were being watched.

We couldn't see anything lurking around us, or some pack of wolves circling us in the night, but for some strange reason we simply could not press on. We both stood there for a long while, and I remember the muscles tingling in my leg. We were both ready to make a decision to either go or leave but just felt the need to observe… Or perhaps we were too afraid to make a move.

Just as I began to purse my lips and speak to my sister about heading back to the car, a large energy shift, accompanied by a growling scream, came from inside the forest. It was as if a low burst of cold wind moved through the trees and clashed against our bodies. The closest I can describe the sound is to compare it to that of a fast, heavy car stopping hard over gravel. It was like a low predatory growl. It was an energy that had an evil momentum almost pushing us from moving forward. The noise was so evil and unnerving, and far from being a human or animal sound, that we instinctively ran as fast as we could toward the car. It was like on an impulse; we just turned and ran.

Just as my fingertips grabbed the handle to the rear car door, the noise screamed again at our heels. I could feel the goose bumps shiver up my spine to the base of my neck as I tucked my feet into the car. It wasn't anything I could make out, but it sounded as if it was right over my shoulder. There might as well have been a two-ton gorilla howling just beyond the car.

My sister's boyfriend started driving in reverse at the sheer response of our frantic entrance into the car. It wasn't until we had completely escaped Coffey Road and were back out on the main stretch that we even stopped the car to catch our breaths. We were huffing, coughing, and could barely get out a word.

"What the heck just happened?" he asked.

"I have no idea what that was, but it was loud!"

"I didn't hear anything; I just saw you two running like bats out of hell," he said.

"You didn't hear that noise? It was only about the scariest thing I have ever heard!" My sister and I both stared at each other and then looked at him. We were in complete disbelief. He honestly had not heard anything. My sister and I, however, had heard the same bloodcurdling growl and didn't see anything to accompany it.

We lowered our blood pressure over some late-night pancakes and talked all night about the old tales of Coffey Road.

Now, years later, we have Google at our fingertips, but still can't find anything linking back to Coffey Road or its gruesome history. We did, however, find some interesting information about quarry mining and government contracting in that area. We learned through some local history research that this acreage of land is also accompanied by UFO sightings. Strange lights, strange stories, and now, no public access.

We were excited to learn that there were strange happenings associated with Coffey Road. Despite her boyfriend's disbelief and lack of validation, my sister and I knew something strange had happened that night. The entire following week was a rehabilitation from one of the most unique paranormal experiences we'd had to date. We didn't even listen to our tape recorders for nearly a week after that event.

All the excitement had dissipated, and my curiosity was gone, but still I sat through thirty-six minutes of boring audio. I suppose I didn't care if something did pop out in the audio or not; I had come to terms with the fact something was unsettling with that land. Just as I had grown tired of listening to the mediocre conversation and bustling of leaves against my jeans, I heard it. The silence. Tick tick tick tick tick.

The tape grew quiet, which almost lead me to believe that the tape had run out. It was the moment we had stood so still in the deep woods that night. Tick, tick, tick, the tape was rolling…

"Grrrrraaaaawwwwwooooowwwwwlllll!" followed by the hasty running back through the forest over broken limbs and heavy breathing. I clicked the tape off.

It had happened.

Coffey Conspiracy?

I had moved out of state not long after I graduated college, but I would often look back on the haunted Coffey Road experience, as there were particular milestones that have reared their heads throughout my paranormal adventures. One of which is the large amount of UFO sightings and visual anomalies associated with haunted locations.

A more popular cultural phenomenon wherein you see the two coupled together is the Mothman. For individuals who have experienced the spiritual omen of the hybrid winged creature with glowing red eyes, headlines usually also are accompanied by strange sightings of UFOs in the nearby area. You see, I had noticed that some of the highest amounts of unidentified flying objects and strange lights in the Parkville area were associated to the same heavy forest that was home to Coffey Road. I found it to be an interesting correlation.

Another interesting note is that currently Coffey Road is only accessible to authorized personnel and is heavily gated from the trespassing of anyone through the heart of Coffey Road. You can drive back about half a mile and then you reach a heavily armored gate and a slew of red signs telling you to stop and go no further. I had begun to wonder who was "authorized."

Coffey Road is now a privately owned location with no street views but has an interesting satellite image when looking at it on Google maps or any other mapping satellite view; it seems to be a quarry or mine. After having reached out to some professionals in and around the mining area of the river basin, it seems to be a limestone quarry; limestone is one of the most heavily abundant minerals in and around this particular stretch of the Missouri River. Not only are there large amounts of limestone, said to be a paranormal conductor, but there is also a large flowing water source within a mile of the Coffey Road area. Many researchers within the paranormal field, religious or otherwise, believe that water is a paranormal conductor because it is an energy conductor; that it quite literally amplifies a presence. Visual and auditory hallucinations are more vivid around the presence of water, and we see the use of water as a metaphorical imagery throughout many religious stories: Holy water, baptisms, cleansings, crossing over the river, the River Jordan, and so forth.

Again, I don't believe in coincidences, but perhaps there might be some deeper meaning to Coffey Road and its strange happenings.

SEVEN

We Call It
Spooky Street

Though my father always could tell a tall tale, he was not one to joke about spiritual matters. I don't know if it was the constant unconscious fear of superstitious beliefs my mother infringed upon him or his deep-rooted Baptist upbringing, but to Dad, spirits were no laughing matter.

Even though my father was the one responsible for the history behind Coffey Road, which is what made it such a spooky story, he did not encourage anything paranormal or joke much about it. There was one story that my dad would tell, and that was about the house up the street. This story did not come about at campfires, or after a late-night Halloween special, but instead was always a warning to us children not to venture our way up "Spooky Street." Uniquely enough, the legend has grown in my mind I'm sure, and the house has since been torn down so there's no way to know for sure... But I do know I still get a little nervous when I drive down Spooky Street.

The first time I heard this house come up in conversation was at the young age of six or seven. My sister and I played with two other little girls our age who were daughters of our dad's friend Rick. I was at the age that Ashley and I would chase our older sisters everywhere they went, and mostly they were on a journey to lose us! We giggled, we caught bugs, we went swimming, and only came into the house when we needed a snack or drink. Their dad, Rick, was a real estate agent, and also a very religious man. That day we had ventured inside for an afternoon lunch and I remember the adults talking at the dinner table. The conversation between Rick and my father was about a house up the street with these crazy occurrences that kept homeowners going in and out like a rotary entrance to an old hotel. He just couldn't seem to figure out what was going on and was unsure of its history.

Rick explained that all sorts of strange stories were coming from the new homeowners and it had since become a thorn in Rick's side. My dad questioned Rick on why all the ruckus; what were these strange occurrences? Rick illustrated that each couple would move into the home and shortly thereafter be calling to see about homeowners' refund policies. Some couples experienced sleepless nights full of clanging and loud noises while others had their electronic devices turning off and on. One couple recently said they had the scariest experience of their lives, though did not give any details of the experience. They simply took a big hit on a short sale and left.

Everyone who bought this house couldn't wait to get out of it after spending no more than a few nights in the home. Of course my mother and her girlfriends were anxious to experience this haunted house and tried to convince Rick to let them explore the home.

"C'mon Rick, what harm will it do? Give us the keys and see if we can't shake up some spirits for you!" my mom laughed.

It was currently vacant, and he was continuing to find plausible explanations for the home and its strange happenings. Rick took a sip of his iced tea and tried to ignore my mother and her cackles about the haunted house, and we all went on with our afternoon. The house was simply growing into a personal nightmare for Rick and a curiosity for those around him.

Just Down the Road

Fast-forward a few years later, when I was old enough to hear more than just bits and pieces of the conversation. I was around nine years old and had grown terribly interested in the paranormal (as my older sister was out with friends doing "high school things" with great stories of her own!). We drove down the road away from home to get some groceries and horse feed, and my dad had taken the sharp left onto Spooky Street; I held my breath as usual. As I sat in the backseat holding in my hot breath, cheeks becoming sore, it caused the eruption of this old memory and I asked my father about the house coming up on the road…the old haunted house on Spooky Street. I included him in on the details of the discussion I remember him having with Rick all those years ago and asked him if there had been any truth to the story. My dad took a deep sigh, and then further explained that he and our mom had actually gone into the home while it was vacant. He remembered that my mom had haggled Rick to the point of going out that very weekend to visit the old home.

He told of a story where he and my mom had ventured up the street late one night with Rick and a few friends. They had entered the home and quickly scattered in the night to find a dark room all alone and possibly have a paranormal experience of their own. My dad skeptically waited in the living room and was hoping in part my mom would, and would not, have an experience that would scare her. No one came bursting out of their empty rooms in the dark very quickly. My dad stood there for minutes, more minutes... long enough that minutes turned to almost an hour. It was then he began to hear a strange noise in the far corner of the room. He called out to the participants there that night and no one answered. He walked further to the corner of the room in the open living space and discovered that there was nothing there. Nothing but some dust and shadows.

Just as he turned to walk away and laugh off the experience, he heard the noise again. This time, the noise was much closer to him and it seemed like it was coming from the corner he had just returned from. My father knew that nothing had scared him and he rationally investigated the corner of the house... Nothing was there. No one had entered the room, no footsteps breezed past him, and yet he heard this noise behind him. As he slowly turned around, he felt a cool breeze on his neck and stared into the dark again only to hear silence. My father stood there and waited. He waited some more. Then, just as he had come back to a rational place again, wondering what he could have possibly heard, the voice of an old woman spoke out from the corner. She called out to him in a pitiful but eerie old voice that made his skin crawl. He knew there was no old woman in the house.

It was then my father broke character and I could see him struggling to complete the story. He put his face in his hands... and his hands then reached back to grab the stressed muscles of his neck. He let a deep breath out...

He explained that he heard a strange old woman's voice speaking to him no more than a foot in front of his face. No one was in the room, nothing was in view, and yet he knew he had clearly heard this voice speaking to him. He explained that the scariest part about the experience was that the rationality of it left him questioning his own mental health. He had explained to my mother on the way home what he had heard, and she didn't much believe him.

My father didn't really speak much about the experience he had at the house that night, but he never did go back to the house. Rick also never sold it. My dad didn't explain what the woman had said to him; I was too scared seeing my dad react so strongly. You never want to see your own father, the pillar of strength, recoiling with fear.

Another Tale

A year later, my mother and I were driving to the grocery store. From our house we would drive up a long street where there was a straightaway to the back of the grocery store, but my mother took a detour this day; I believe it was most likely to finish her cigarette as she drove. Regardless of the reason why, she turned down Spooky Street.

We never drove down the street, and if we did, everyone in the car seemed uneasy. The street itself isn't scary; in fact, it's very green and full of fresh foliage. As you drive 35 mph the homes creep up on you; all of the homes have beautiful welcoming front porches adorned with flowers and pots. You turn a bend, creep around the corner, and there on the left sits the small white house. No one was ever playing in the front yard or enjoying the property, though there were at least five lush green acres of a horse field stretching over the property. You never caught anyone walking from the front door to their car; in fact no cars were ever parked in the driveway. This little white house on the left was what gave Spooky Street its name. This was the house Rick could never sell. This was the house where my dad had that very creepy paranormal experience. This was the house that put a crack in the illustration of my father I had always kept so tightly guarded in my mind. It was a simple house.

I broke the anxiety in the air with a question I formed as a joke. "So do you think Rick ever sold that house?" My mother, who always had a sick sense of humor, whipped a look of dismay back at me over her shoulder.

"You know Rick died, don't you?" As she said it, I instantly felt guilty. By the age of ten, I had been to more than ten funerals. My mother and father were quite popular and had a large group of friends. My dad was part of a motorcycle group and my mom was a musician. Funerals weren't terribly common, but I had almost forgotten Rick's. I suppose as my mother reminded me, I did indeed know Rick had passed. I remember his funeral well. His two daughters, the same age as my sister and I, cried in the front pew. I didn't even know it was Rick until after the funeral and asked. People never look the way they do alive as they do dead in their casket. I hadn't recognized him. This memory shot back into my present like a pellet gun. Sharp, painful, and annoying. I slumped back in my seat, "I'm sorry. That's right, I forgot."

"It is funny that you mention that though, because it was this house that killed him."

Of course, my guilt of bringing up such a sour subject in the form of a joke made me completely forget about my intentions for asking at all in the first place. I unconsciously itched to know more about this house on Spooky Street. My mother was about to tell me more. "That almost put him under, that damn house," she laughed. "He tried to sell it so many times and even turned to an exorcist, he was so desperate."

I barely heard the leather squeaking underneath me in the hot sun as I inched to the edge of the bucket seat to know more. "What's that? An exorcist?"

"Of course," she laughed, "so many damn people complained about hearing and seeing stuff in that house he didn't know what else to do. Not to mention the fact that your dad and I had our own experience in the creepy place. Your dad still doesn't talk much about it, fucking old woman nearly turned him sheet white!" My mother always did have a crass way of illustrating things, but she was right. The experience in the house had changed my dad and the way he saw the paranormal.

"Well, what happened with the exorcist? What did he tell you?" I bugged and bothered.

My mom took a big drag off her cigarette as it hung between her lips, chapped in old lipstick. She grinned and blew the smoke from her mouth; I wanted the story to escape from her just as the smoke had instantly been sucked to the outside.

"He called in a friend of a friend who knew someone with the Baptist Church that would come out and bless the place. He didn't just bless it though, Rick said he felt the need to exorcise the house, which I didn't even think they did! But…I can see why someone would feel the need to cleanse that house, some serious shit lives there."

She reached down to the radio and her cigarette hissed as her breath kick-started the flame; the volume increased. She did whisper over her shoulder before she tuned out, "Exorcisms do usually kill people."

I slunk back into the worn leather bucket seat in the back and peered out the window. The house on Spooky Street was nearly a few miles back now, but still it lingered in my thoughts.

Spooky Street and that creepy old house hadn't just scared my dad from his faith, stressed a man to his early grave, or put fear into my heart enough to induce nightmares, but it had also terrified my sister and me on a few occasions. Now, I'm the first one to consider the power of suggestion, but this house truly had a reputation. I must have been past this house and down Spooky Street a thousand times, and though nothing usually happened, the handful of truly terrifying things that have happened is more than a coincidence to make me believe, and know, that something lurks on the property of that little white house.

Body Bags

It was a normal afternoon in the hot Missouri summer. Just after waking from a hot, sticky nap, I waited for my sister to arrive home from a friend's house. Looking back, I was five or six and my sister was a young prepubescent teen that hated nothing more than to be bothered by her little sister, so I often waited by the door to annoy her when she came home. This day, however, just before the lightning bugs were to light up the yard at sundown, she came pedaling up the driveway as quick as her legs could take her. She buzzed past me and my petty comment about her being late and ran into the house through the loud screen door. The door slammed at her heels before I could even inch behind her, but I could already hear her screaming for Mom in the kitchen. I followed behind her into the old kitchen, out to the backyard, and into our garden by the shed. Mom was picking veggies from the garden and placing them into a laundry hamper for easy rinsing with the garden hose. My sister ran to her side screaming, "I hope it isn't someone's cat mom, but you have to come see!"

I couldn't figure out what she was babbling to Mom, but she clearly had an interest in something up the road. "Just as you turn up onto Spooky Street, Mom, Christy and I kept seeing these black bags on the road like someone had picked up litter, you know, like we did in Campfire Girls! But Mom, they were really smelly and each time we biked by we could smell this horrible stench, like a garbage can or something. Then one was kind of open and we stopped to see what it was and, oh my God, Mom, would you believe it was someone's pet!? Someone didn't bury their pet and put it in a trash bag! It seriously is so gross and there are like three of them!"

My sister kept squealing for my mom to drive up and see.

"Should we call the cops or maybe bury the poor things? Do you think Dad would dig a hole in our yard to bury them?" My sister cried on and on. My mom hushed my sister to calm down and assured her that we would not be burying the animals in our yard and that it probably was the city picking up road kill or maybe it was someone's trash and they had butchered a recent deer or something on their property and dispersed the bags in front of others' yards in case they'd get in trouble. My mom exaggerated a few plausible tales about why such bags of rotten flesh would be littering the street and that we had better things to do than go get covered in maggots on a hot summer night. Plus, we were going to catch fireflies!

That night after the sun had tucked behind the horizon, and the fireflies had all been captured and smeared onto the cement out front and the glowing entrails had lost their luster, the news came on. A horrible story of how an unidentified missing person had been discovered in pieces on the side of a suburban residential street. Their body cut limb from limb and disposed of in a simple dirty black trash bag trail that littered the road for nearly a mile. At least three news channels were carrying the story, but none gave details to the exact road, the person found, or how it all came to be. It was as open-ended and mysterious as Spooky Street itself, and though the newscaster didn't say Parkville, Missouri, we knew just where the horrific tragedy had happened.

My sister didn't finish her dinner that night and left her Heathcliff TV tray half full of her remaining dinner and ice cream. My sister often recoiled from any social situation back into the depths of her corner bedroom at the end of the hall, but tonight we knew she wasn't buried in a fantasy book or Depeche Mode cassette tape but instead was trying to find peace. The peace to lie on her pillow and find sleep when knowing just up a mile from the house was the entrance to Spooky Street.

A Carcass Under the Car

That wasn't the only time Spooky Street had haunted my sister. Though you could take as many as six different ways through the residential neighborhoods to get to the local high school, Spooky Street was the most direct path. Regardless of it being an efficient route, my sister (and later I, when I was of driving age) rarely took Spooky Street if we didn't have to. This morning, however, my sister was late for school. She was in drama, an honor student in sciences, and played flute in the band.

She was too late to grab breakfast, too late to say good-bye to the family, and definitely too late to not take Spooky Street to make up five minutes.

She drove down the winding, wooded road, which was still dusted with morning dew and fog. As the street bent to the little white house, you find yourself in a blind spot to oncoming and ongoing traffic and for a moment you are alone with yourself, your car, and a straight view of the haunted house on Spooky Street. Sometimes you find yourself unaware of the road as you're lost in your thoughts; the direct view often stealing your focus for a moment and seizing your attention. Just as my sister was caught in this brief moment of unconscious gloom, her car came to a screeching halt.

"Grrruwuwuwlalawawla clang." Something drug under her car.

Like claws from underneath the car came a loud, sharp sound that made her toggle her hands between controlling the steering wheel and covering her ears. The car finally came to a stop and where one might immediately jump from the car to see what had happened, my sister sat in fear as she realized she and her car were now paralyzed outside on the road, in the fog, just feet from the little white house on Spooky Street. In a time without cell phones to call for help, she pondered what to do. Her heart was pounding and in a place of fear.

She turned the key and the car started. A sigh of relief and warm, safe anticipation moved over her as she put the car into gear and pressed the gas; she would inspect the car when she got to school. After all, there was no one, no cars, and that noise couldn't have been a deer. As she pressed down on the accelerator, the car hissed and squealed again, and she pressed the brakes to stop the sound; it was like nails on a chalkboard and she could feel the sting in her feet as it moved through the car. Something was underneath. Here she was, usually too afraid to breathe when driving past this stretch of road and now she was going to have to get out and see what was under the car.

She wiped the sweat from her hands and quickly jolted from the seat to outside the car where she gathered her strength to get down on her knees. She inhaled, closed her eyes, and then calmly got down on her hands and knees to look below her small compact car.

She looked and couldn't see well what the object was, but it was big. Could it be someone's bumper or something left in the road from someone's pickup? Maybe someone had dropped something during a move. She reached her hand underneath, just beyond the shadow of her undercarriage to touch the object. If it were soft or malleable she could just drive over it, but if it was something else she might have to back off and try again. Reaching quickly so that she could assess the issue and get to school (and keep from getting hit by any other traffic) she stretched her hand to the object and touched it and … it was wet! She recoiled her hand back to her body like a whip and looked down in horror to what looked like blood. She looked again under the car and she began to make out the details of some sort of carcass between the tires.

The object could have been a cow, a horse, some type of farm animal, but out here in the middle of a wooded residential street? Why could she see the skeleton as if it had been rotting for weeks and yet the flesh was still bleeding red blood? She wiped the mess on her jeans and quickly got back into her car. She wiped the tears of worry from her wet cheeks and cranked the key once more to start the ignition. She slammed on the gas pedal, regardless of what damage it might cause, and spun out over the rest of the carcass that lay beneath the automobile. She gained traction and peeled out...leaving the body in the street. She wasn't sure what it was but she knew she wasn't going to spend another moment on that road outside the little white house and had no interest in anything that could follow her to school or even home. What evil thing could be leaving bodies bloody all over the road? One might ask who lived in that house and perhaps they would call to have it removed, but we all knew, no one lived in that house.

My sister finished out the day at school thinking of nothing but the horrifying experience she had had that morning and how it plummeted her to the dark nights up alone after the body bags incident. She had told her boyfriend, Ian, the whole story and even showed him the damage on the underneath of her car after school. She still had the blood smear on her jeans and was clearly shaken by the incident so Ian agreed to follow her home on Spooky Street to further investigate what it was. They inched along the back road and came upon the little white house and the bend in the road. No body or bloodstain was on the road; there was nothing but a normal patch of pavement stretched onward around the wooded bend. My sister was even more terrified as it seemed the whole thing had happened just in her imagination, yet the evidence of her fear was still stained onto her pants and scratched into her car.

There was no explanation as the conclusion again lay open-ended and mysterious, as most happenings on Spooky Street had. I can tell you that I still get a little uneasy when driving down Spooky Street, whether it is in the daytime or late at night. All the same, I feel my heart jump into my throat and I quickly recollect the slew of scary stories that have happened to all of my family members.

I used to want to go up to the little white house to see if anyone had ever been brave enough to live there beyond a few weeks, and if they would be surprised that I was inquiring about it being haunted. I assumed if someone had lived there they would have countless scary tales to tell, and I had almost conjured up the courage to ask when I learned the house was torn down. It was true, after decades of remaining barren and uninhabited, the property was sold and someone tore down the little white house. Now the front yard and plot is a horse ranch and a much larger home was built back about three hundred feet from where the spooky old house had once stood. I still ponder if some evil energy haunts the home, the horses, or the patch of road along Spooky Street, but I do know the tales of its haunted past are still very much alive.

EIGHT

In My
Grandpa's Skin

We all have one or a few people who have stayed with us after they've passed. That one person who was always connected with you in the living, and after their passing the grief remained for some time, or lingers on for years. For me, that was my Grandpa Harmon. He was a kind man of few words and could always be found in the workshop under his work light late at night. He was a hard worker, a gentle soul, and I miss him dearly.

He had passed unexpectedly, though it was on my grandmother's birthday so we all had talked to Grandpa that night and shared our blessings with him. I had just graduated high school and was living out on my own when I got the call of his passing. He was wise beyond his years and perhaps used that night as one of closure. After saying "I love yous" to everyone, he let go in his sleep. I believe he always had a plan and

95

was always thinking of others in his heart. I had spoken to him no more than an hour before he passed that evening, and though I was at peace having said my goodbyes, I wish I could have had more time with my grandpa. He was very special and dear to me.

At his funeral I could barely keep myself together. It wasn't until I stood at his casket and his skin was no longer pink and alive that it really hit me. He was gone. No more walking trails, carving walking sticks, or snacking on cinnamon in the garden. No more pruning roses or plucking mulberries while on his shoulders, or requests to change the wheel on my scooter he kept hung in the garage for the grandkids. No more fiddle playing, smashed coins on the train tracks made into jewelry, or fun wooden puzzles he made for us.

I missed so much about him, and standing over his casket made it cold and true that his time had passed against my will; I wasn't ready to say goodbye. As I approached my dad to hug him I could feel the lump in my throat building. I couldn't say anything, I couldn't find words. I then hugged my stepmom and just let go. I cried like one does in the shower, when no one is around, when you're pints-deep in ice cream post social tragedy. I didn't have room for embarrassment in my heart or mind and the snot, tears, and makeup streaming down my face was just there, amidst the despair and sadness I felt. I wanted to celebrate his life and he had requested we do so at his funeral, and damn me if I couldn't muster the respect to smile.

I went out to my car, and after the door closed me alone in the silence, I cried again. The procession was going to bury him, and I didn't turn on my car, I didn't move. I spoke out to my grandfather that if he were present, if he could hear me, I couldn't live without him in my life. I needed him.

Just then I looked up at the bush in front of my car; just before the gravestones, and after the crumbling asphalt, was a cardinal. My windshield was foggy and littered with bug pieces, but through the light rain I could see it, perched right at my eye level. You see, my grandfather loved to feed his birds and share his knowledge of nature with all the grandkids. He would whittle us a walking stick and Grandma would pack a lunch as we headed out to spend the day in some nature sanctuary. Through the walking trails and hiking paths he would point out trees, plants, animals, and birds, and teach me all about them. Each morning and at every meal throughout the day, Grandpa's roses and the line of birdfeeders could be seen from the large window in the kitchen. The birds would join us, and as we ate our food, we could watch them peck and flutter. If there was one I didn't recognize Grandpa would always point to his books to show me a new bird.

I loved blue jays. They were always the bad guys in the bedtime stories Grandma read to me, but I loved their bright colors and decorated wings. Grandpa always loved the cardinals. I started a running inside joke with him on one of our trails when I pointed at a cardinal and said, "Look Grandpa, a red jay!" We laughed as he corrected me, and after that we would always point out the red jays together and giggle. I drew him cardinals in my cards and he would sketch or whittle them into the gifts he gave me.

Now as I sat in my car, there in the bush was a cardinal, just as I would always point out to him. I did find a smile in all the sadness at the present he had sent me; a sign that he was still with me.

I was always wondering how that would work for him and his spirit, because he was a devout Christian so I knew he had planned and prayed to be in heaven alongside God. I didn't know if I could believe he would visit me in the form of a bird, so just in case I had any doubt, I called out to the red jay, "That's you Grandpa. I see you. Anytime I need you, or you need me, just show me a cardinal and I'll know you're here."

Synchronicity or coincidence aside, I usually see cardinals just when Grandpa would be present: after the birth of my first son, at my grandma's birthday, on family outings to the zoo, or out walking on a trail. Though I would love for my grandpa to visit me in another form, I know this is what works for us.

That is why the one true time I know I saw a demon, I learned the true feeling of evil.

My Haunted Duplex

I had moved into a duplex up the street from my family home; Grandpa had been gone for two years and I still wanted to be close to home. I moved to a place just two turns down Spooky Street and two miles from the haunted house I had grown up in. In my backyard was the football field for the local high school.

The duplex wasn't old, but it wasn't new, and I had enjoyed repainting the walls and redoing the landscaping to make it my own. Within a few weeks of moving in I began to hear noises and creaks, and though some of the sounds could be written off as being natural sounds, or even the strange neighbors, somewhere "something else" was making some noises, too... but I was used to that.

Eventually items started to move or go missing. I then decided I didn't want to be alone in the duplex all the time. I had found a small cat in a box outside a local retail store, so I rescued the white fluff ball and he enjoyed having his dominion in the duplex. He was barely six weeks old and grew to hate everyone but me and my then-boyfriend. Cedric was also my little guardian cat and would hiss and growl at anything I questioned. It became a sense of validation for me.

One day I had my sister and friends over to help with some wrapping of gifts for a wedding when the lights flickered on and off. My sister laughed, "Is that your ghost you've been talking about?!"

Some of my girlfriends paused in fear and I answered, "Yes, but that is not all he does." I raised my eyebrow and winked at my sister as the other girls shifted in their seats. I encouraged them to go into the kitchen and take a look if they didn't believe me.

I had gotten so used to the fact that when the lights flickered it almost always meant the ghost had been in my kitchen and that something in that room would have occurred. The cabinets and drawers, without noise or force, would all be open. I never heard the occurrence but it happened weekly. I didn't get a bad feeling; nothing ever scratched me, and I didn't have nightmares or strange gut reactions, and the occasional hiss from Cedric was not keeping me up at night. Coming from a house that had an old woman haunting it, someone who actually had appeared to me, a few open cabinet doors were the least of my worries, and it became a fun trick to scare off friends or neighbors.

I even asked the landlord if they had experienced this and they seemed offended I had asked such a question. They didn't give me a definitive answer, but regardless, it wasn't going to scare me away, because the rent was great!

One morning, like any other, I waved bye to my boyfriend and turned on my Pandora music, blaring through the house. I cleaned up after breakfast and danced my way down the hall and into my bathroom at the end of the hall to prepare for the day. The upper level was almost like an "H," with one area being a large, open living room and then a long hallway connected the three rooms at the end of the hall; the bathroom was the middle room. Even sitting on the toilet I could see all the way to the farthest wall in the living room. Cedric loved to spazz out on the stretch of carpet.

I danced on the old tile floor and slathered toothpaste on my toothbrush. In just boxer brief shorts and a tank top, I began to brush my teeth when I saw something out of the corner of my eye. I didn't panic but stood still for a moment and looked shyly through my peripheral vision. I didn't see anything. Perhaps it was the cat, perhaps I was seeing things... though it did seem dark and tall. Maybe my boyfriend had forgotten his tie again and was running in to grab something. I went back to my morning routine.

I then saw the figure again, tall and dark at the end of the hall, but this time it didn't flutter by. It stood like a floater in the corner of my eye and my stomach suddenly dropped. I kept brushing my teeth and I looked into the mirror thinking, "Okay Sarah, this is the time the ghost is going to show himself. We know it's a man, we know he plays in the kitchen, but he is not mean or negative. No worries." I continued the pep talk, but my stomach began to turn as the "creature" started to move and twitch at the end of the hall. It was slender, black, and featureless.

"Sarah," I thought to myself, "be strong. Be grounded. White lights and positive energy. You are protected and you have experience with this sort of thing. Talk with it, tell it your boundaries, and get on with it." I repeated this in my head and took a deep breath. Just as I began to feel strong and back to my normal self, despite the figure still lurking in my peripheral vision, I couldn't help but notice the nausea kick in. I spit out my foamy, used toothpaste and wiped my face with a towel, then turned my back to the hall to grab my hairbrush. Perhaps if I didn't care, it would just go away. When I turned back to the mirror, the figure had gotten closer, but stopped as I noticed it. It knew what I was thinking.

"Okay, look at it. Sarah. Just look!" Despite the intuition to just go on with my day and ignore the sickness growing in my stomach, I closed my eyes to gather the strength to turn around and face this creature. I turned my body, faced my toes toward the end of the hall, and envisioned my protective bubble. I swallowed slowly and tried to relax my tightened facial muscles; I was terrified. "Deep breath…" I thought, "Just open your eyes."

I opened my eyes.

There, at the end of the hallway, the tall dark figure had vanished, but the image of my grandfather was there instead. I immediately cried and gasped with surprise. I put my hand over my heart and a sigh of relief moved over me as I was finally getting a visitation from my beloved grandpa. "I miss you, Grandpa!" the thoughts moving to my lips … Just as I wiped the tears from my eyes and moved toward my grandpa, my intuition stopped me at the divider on the floor. A golden plastic boundary in the floor like a spiritual line in the sand. Just where the small three-by-five bathroom tile met the carpet, I seemed to freeze. I thought for a moment and refocused to the apparition at the end of the hall. There, just above the stairs, no more than fifteen feet from me was my grandpa. It wasn't fuzzy, it wasn't see-through or wispy, it was a clear and solid figure of my grandpa smiling back at me. I called out to him, "Grandpa, I've missed you so much! I'm so glad, so honored. Do you hear me?"

Demonic Jabberwocky

I had spoken with spirits and communicated with ghosts, but never had I seen the full embodiment of a dear loved one. I had prayed for such a thing! Usually with the visitation of a spirit I see images, as if getting uploaded with memories that aren't mine, so that I can convey bits and pieces to those around me. I've had dreams, heard voices, but never actually stood face-to-face with an apparition of someone I knew.

Usually I have a strong sense of myself and can feel separated and strong in the presence of a ghost; guarded and protected. This time, however, it was different. I felt lost, alone, somewhat scared—I wasn't getting any images, memories, thoughts. I wasn't even getting recollections of my missed moments with Grandpa, but was instead fixated on the figure that stood before me. I couldn't help but stare at the face; something was off. "Grandpa, do you hear me? Is that you?"

The face was just a fixed smile, unnatural and frozen, and the eyes... they weren't right. My grandpa had kind eyes with crow's feet that decorated his face from all the years of smiling. I remember his callused hands, his smell of wood shavings and cologne, and his body language. This figure seemed empty, unhappy, unhinged.

Just as I called out to him again his head twitched to the side as if water was in his ears. Not in a human turn of the neck, but in a glitch, as if bones were breaking beneath the skin. This awkward movement scared me and I began to notice that this was not my grandpa. The eyes weren't kind, there was no character or soul... but something else. My skin grew cold, my stomach was turning, and I felt as if I was going to puke. Yet I felt so overwhelmed with fear that I couldn't take my eyes off the figure; I couldn't even blink. I didn't want the image to change, to disappear. I stared at the creature masquerading as my grandpa, and it began to move toward me. It didn't take a step with feet, like a person would if walking down the hall. Instead it was just moving, and the entire bottom half of the body didn't actually step as it inched towards me; it was just drawing nearer as if it were on a motorized platform.

The face was drawn to my eyes and locked in on me and the neck was broken to the left. It moved like an old puppet on strings or in an old mechanical puppet show, and as it crept closer I felt dread. I felt fear, I felt evil, and I didn't know what to do or how to escape it. I didn't want to close my eyes, but I didn't want to see it moving toward me either, so I backed my body into the bathroom as far as I could go and curled up against the tile of the bathtub at my back. With my arms wrapped tightly around my knees and my body tucked as tightly as it would go, I braced myself for the creature to loom over me. It was so close I could nearly reach out to it. Just as the figure crept to the bathroom doorway and walked into the bathroom light, it stopped, just as I had done trying to walk out into the hall before. I felt a horrible knot in my throat as I called out, "Why are you doing this! You're not my grandpa, go away!"

The creature put its arms on the doorway and leaned its ribcage as far as it could go. The arms were thin and out-stretched in the awning of the doorway, and I could see the skin tightening around the bones in its neck. As it moved into the bathroom light, I could see that though it still looked like my grandpa, his soft buttoned shirt against jeans, the crea-ture was wet underneath, and the clothing was sticky in some places. There was no breathing, but every few moments I could see the stains of something underneath the clothing spilling through. The head coiled around, like a ball joint loose on a pivot, and the face gawked at me. It took a deep breath in, without blinking, and stared right at me, and then the jaw seemed to unhinge. I took a deep breath in, holding back tears, I simply braced myself. The figure opened its mouth and out of this gaping blackness in its face...screamed at me, like the wailing of a small animal at the top of its lungs. The sound struck me hard with fright, and I brought my knees tightly to my chest. The face of my grandfather melted into the distorted, long jawline and dark eye sockets of this creature as it smiled down at me. It was happy I had been deceived and it was happy my terror was unbearable.

I couldn't do anything, but felt some relief that for whatever reason, the creature didn't enter the bathroom where I lay in the tight ball on the floor. Eventually, after what seemed like an eternity, I broke my gaze from this creature and sobbed. I cried by myself in a ball on the floor. Eventually it wasn't there when I looked up.

I prayed. I cried. I buried my head in my lap and stayed in the bathroom all day. I didn't dare cross the threshold into my hallway and onto the carpet knowing that something was in the house so evil that it dare appear as my grandpa.

I had never felt so sick, weak, ill, and taken by an entity in all my experiences with the paranormal. When I look back on the scenario now, I realize that it took the image of a loved one to gain my trust and catch me off guard. Had I truly believed it was my grandfather, I would have opened up my soul to have that connection again. Evil knows this.

I believe in energy and a balance in nature. Where there is pure love and goodness there is also a dark sadness and evil that awaits in the shadows to bring balance to our world. I know such a thing exists but had never experienced it firsthand in my own home; it was life-changing.

I am unsure if demons really do exist, in the religious sense of the word, but I know my grandfather was a Christian and did believe in demons. I feel after this experience that maybe demons do walk this plane and malinger about the living. One thing is for certain, I moved from that duplex shortly thereafter and luckily have not had a visit from this creature since.

NINE

It Came Home
from the Hospital

I had experienced my one, okay maybe two, run-ins with something I could agree possibly being demonic or truly evil—the demon-creature at my duplex, the shadow figures and strange happenings—but I hardly believed in attachments. But I began to wonder... did pieces of these things stick to us and ride along? I personally believe that spiritual entities are somehow bound for some reason, otherwise why would they be here? If they are conscience entities lingering with issues from their most recent physical life here on earth, there is some reason they appear when and where they do; otherwise, why the attachment?

Attachments are usually discussed in whispers as some demonic or evil entity that sees you on the ghost tour or residential case and finds your weakness. Maybe you came into the situation stressed, tired, drugged, unempathetic, or too empathetic, and it attached to you long after the investigation was complete.

Why then would you not pick up attachments all day every day? I have a bad day at least once a month, so why am I not picking up attachments on those days and accumulating negative spirits like a bag lady? Some psychics, energy workers, and shamans agree that I am, in some ways, doing just this. Cancer, stress, anxiety… it all compounds in some way from the world around us and if we don't remedy this buildup of negative energy then it can overcome and control our lives. Perhaps that's why attachments are associated with demons.

What or who is to say what is right or wrong? At this point in the paranormal game, no one is validated completely by scientific evidence and even if quantum energy and scientific theories prove energy transfer, the spiritual attachment debate is still out.

But I do know that something came home with me from that hospital; no doubt in my mind about that.

The Patient

I have investigated in more than eleven countries, thirty-eight states in the nation, and more than three continents: Old castles, the most horrific places in London, and historically bloody battlegrounds, but it was this old hospital in the Midwest that had called to me most of my life. If it came up in conversation or on a television special, I was drawn to it like a moth to a flame.

It had been a tuberculosis hospital that saw an amazing amount of death in its peak, and the legends of the hauntings rang loudly in the paranormal community. In 2008 I took a trip alongside a paranormal conference to this hospital and was excited to be doing some parapsychology research at such a hotspot for paranormal happenings. Not only was this hospital notorious for its activity, but it was also a massive structure rising out of the woods—a great place to gather decent evidence without much pollution from traffic, city lights, or surrounding gadgets.

A small group of people would be investigating the location for three days, and I was attending the investigation with a very dear friend and experienced pastor. Not only did I have a pastor at my side, friends over my shoulder, and a great deal of equipment, but I was in good spirits. I was going through a very turbulent time in my relationship at home and the chance to investigate a monumental structure in the mental health history records was a great vacation I was looking forward to enjoying.

I spent most of the day upon my arrival mingling with friends I hadn't seen in some time. We ate great food in the lobby, drank some refreshments, and laughed out on the patio as a guest investigator played some music late into the night. Two close girlfriends and I giggled our way to the room where I snuggled into my cot on the floor. The next day I attended workshops, gave a lecture, and had lunch with fellow investigators, and we all excitedly gathered our equipment in preparation for the first night at the hospital. I did some quick exercises before the night's events, such as grounding, visualizations, and even stocking my pockets with some totems of mine. My dear friend Christine insisted on commenting, "Don't bring anything back now!"

I laughed as I closed the door behind me and ran to my car. Christine was staying behind and I had to drive out to the hospital by myself that night. I drove the fifteen miles to the hospital and waved to the owner as I passed through the welcoming iron gates. I parked my car in the gravel area outside the safe house and joined my team for a friendly auction and workshop on the hospital's history.

I spent the rest of the night gathering evidence for my parapsychology research in just one small room on the first floor of the hospital with the God Helmet. The God Helmet is a gadget created by a neuroscientist by the name of Koren in hopes of stimulating the temporal lobes and heightening paranormal sensation. I wore the God Helmet in conjunction with blinking strobe lights and headphones that played binaural beats (tones and frequencies used to alter state of consciousness) in hopes of accumulating some interesting findings for my parapsychology research. I hadn't felt any strange sensations, heard any whispers, or even seen some of the many proclaimed "active shadow people." Instead I had been taking notes and recordings with otherwise normal readings. I had a few strange and exciting occurrences with the God Helmet (such as goose bumps and a heightened sense of intuition), but as the night came to a close, nothing too extraordinary.

I gently tucked my wires into my laptop case and gathered all my equipment. I took a few photos of myself and the staff, then sat in my chair back at the safe house with friends as the night came to a close. Staff had dwindled this late in the evening so the event coordinator and staff asked if some of us who remained could each take a floor and make sure any and all guests were cleared before closing up shop. I agreed to help out. After all, I was so excited to have such an iconic haunted hospital at my fingertips.

I took the top floor, home to some of the most horrifying rumors haunting the hospital's history, and was joined by my friend the pastor and his fiancé. We took flashlights to each unlocked patient room and gazed out on the flat fields through the gaping open windows where tuberculosis patients once hoped for recovery. Deep breaths, calm energy, and no ghosts.

No guests or ghouls were hiding, so we took some photos as we descended down to the main corridor on the ground floor. The pastor and his fiancé walked ahead of me as I meandered past the morgue, the cafeteria, and the open office rooms. It was moving to stand in this barren hospital that once had so many people passing from tuberculosis that they used the equipment chute to move bodies; it was a historical heaviness that came over me.

I smiled at my realization that I had investigated it, and though I didn't have a paranormal experience, I was here. I turned to walk the remaining four hundred feet to the safe house down the dark hallway from the morgue to the gift shop area. Just as I passed a room, I heard a clear exclamation...

"Sarah."

I stopped. I took a deep breath in, and immediately calmed my surprise to hear something so clear and loud in the dark, but knew it had to be a friend or guest of the event, because it was clearly a human voice, a vocal shout to me from across the room I had passed. I pivoted and slowly turned back the way the voice had come from and backtracked to the room. I flashed my LED flashlight and saw nothing. No one was in the room, the hallway, behind me, or anywhere on the floor. Immediately my calm energy shifted to an empty feeling of fear.

"Hello," I called out.

I seriously was sure at this point my eyes had deceived me and it was someone left on the floor, but no one called back to me. I walked quickly back down the hall, the way I had been going, toward the safe house, toward light and friends and people.

"Sarah!"

The male voice was louder, it was just behind me and its clear presence put a haste in my step as I pushed further down the hall. I was nearly running by the time I arrived in the safe house, and I rushed to my friends, who were all laughing and gathering their things.

"Did you hear that?" I burst into their conversation and everyone looked blankly at me. I walked over to the owner and explained what had happened and she laughed. She then pointed to the screen of the camera that was aimed on the cafeteria and concluded no one was there.

"Just because nothing is on the camera doesn't mean no one is in there. That man calls out a lot actually, so I'm sure that is who you were dealing with."

I was amazed. I had the paranormal experience I was longing for, but honestly, it was scarier than I had thought it would be. It wasn't a ghoulish figure or the ghost of some suicidal nurse, but instead it the voice of a man who knew my name. The voice wasn't repeating some horrific memory from when it was a slave to a dying body, but instead was calling out from the other side *to me*, by name. The conscience knowledge of my presence, my name, and the fact it waited until I was alone scared me. And my own imagination filling in the gaps of the lack of it showing itself to me was even worse. It was smart, it was intuitive, and that is what piqued my interest most!

I packed up my car and drove over the gravel much faster than when I had arrived at sundown hours earlier. I was relieved to see civilization ahead as the late-night lights of fast food chains littered the highway back to the hotel. Each pedestrian, gas station, pothole brought me back to the secure life I was used to, the one that didn't have voices calling out to me in the dark. I parked the car, rushed from the elevator to my room, and was relieved to be in the sanctuary of my shared room among friends. One friend was fast asleep in her bed while the other sat awake in the twin bed by the window clicking away at the remote. I turned to put my purse down in the makeshift closet and secured the door behind me. As I rounded the corner into the room, Christine turned her head and said, "I thought I told you not to bring anyone back."

I wasn't laughing this time and her words shocked me. How could she know? Was this some sick joke or coincidence? "What do you mean?" I asked.

I peeled off my socks, crawled into my cot, and looked at her with a fake smile I prayed would match her joking manner, but she wasn't joking.

"Sarah, you brought him back with you. Good thing we're going home tomorrow." She turned off the TV, pulled the covers over her shoulders, and turned to face the other wall. I couldn't see if she was hiding a smile that perhaps was proof she had just acted her ass off, but instead I was left with a pit in my stomach; was she right? Had I brought *him* back with me?

An Attachment

It had been months since my visit to the hospital, but things at home hadn't gotten better, in fact they had gotten much worse. I was sour most days and my work was a constant headache. School was a struggle, my relationship was on its last leg, and the news of my grandmother's passing had put me in a very dark place. The thought of the man in the hospital and that dark voice that had called out to me hadn't even crossed my mind until a random message came to me over a social networking site one afternoon.

"Sarah, I just thought you should know that lately your picture has been haunting me. Even though it's the same photo you've had up for some time, I see something else in it these days. Are you okay?"

I scoffed at the nerve of this person who felt the need to spread their psychic hullabaloo toward me via a social site, and just after the death of my grandmother no less. I deleted it.

A few days later I was a guest on a radio show where the live chat streamed online during the radio broadcast. I love when shows have correlating chat rooms, because then I can banter with those listening and have private conversations and debates on the topic of the show for those who are tuning in; it takes the show to a whole new level. During the first break of the radio broadcast, another psychic acquaintance of mine private messaged me:

"Sarah, I thought you should know you have a negative attachment with you. It's been with you now for some time and it is growing stronger. I can even hear it in your voice."

I commented back that I'd have to do some cleansing and quickly discontinued the private message thread. I backed away from the computer screen and finished the show in my living room away from the chat room. I believed and still do believe in psychic workers and energy, but couldn't accept that I did indeed have some attachment near me. I continued to live my life, go to work, eat meals, and just found the incoming random messages from people a bit of a sickening synchronicity. I ignored it as much as I could. The third, the fourth, even the eleventh that week.

Ironic or not, my paranormal team in Columbia, Missouri, at that time had been receiving a slew of negative calls about hauntings. One family had a young son who was seeing an alien in his television screen at night and items were flying across the kitchen, and another young man was having furniture stack itself, and one of his two family dogs had been attacked by "something" that left it to bleed out in his garage, to death.

We decided to take both cases immediately and each one grew more and more terrifying by the day. Finally, the man in Jefferson City, Missouri, needed us to come out immediately to cleanse the home, regardless of the fact we were still reviewing history and evidence. So my team and I gathered as much equipment as we could and began the fifty-mile drive to his home. It was a Tuesday afternoon, great weather, and an empty back highway all the way to the state's capital. I kept thinking the whole way there that I had no idea what to expect. One of his dogs had eaten the other, the neighbors had strange interviews, and here he was needing help in the middle of the afternoon with little-to-no details, just a "Hurry!"

I had only been present for an evil case once, aside from my own run-in with the creature in my duplex nearly two years earlier. I had heard many stories, read many e-mails, but most hauntings were rational experiences that ended up being explained by some logical physical reason. Only one case of mine, in Quincy, Illinois, had been something "else."

I had only left that case three months ago, just after returning from the haunted hospital in Kentucky, and didn't want to revisit anything like that anytime soon. A young girl, despite the combination of mental health issues and larger family issues, had needed an exorcism, and I was asked to help in the therapeutic process before and after the ordeal. The events of this case were quite graphic and I was working on just healing from the energy exerted through the exorcism process. Come to think of it, everything since that hospital had some negative aftertaste to it.

I kept praying that this man in Jefferson City was just misinterpreting something. Just then my car began to clunk and gasp. I looked down at my gauge and the lever was far into the red. Smoke came gushing from my car vents and my cabin was filling up fast with gray smoke that smelled of burnt plastic. I quickly pulled to the shoulder, slammed on the brakes, and jumped from the car alongside the highway. I called my father as quickly as my fingers could dial, because he was a mechanic and perhaps he could put my mind at ease. But he didn't answer. Instead I watched my radiator catch fire and burn under the hood of my recently purchased car. It had never had any issues before and I didn't understand what in the world was happening. I had just spent all my extra savings on the trip home to my grandmother's funeral and I couldn't afford this!

My teammates who were driving behind me on the way to the case pulled over to give me a ride. I called the tow company, my insurance, my parents, and made arrangements for me and my burning car as we arrived at the site of our emergency case.

Rather than finding the young man outside his home, we simply saw an empty driveway, a rusty side gate ajar behind the house, and a neighbor closely watching us from across the street. After no call, no answer, no greeting from either the locked door of the home or the abandoned cell phone of the young man, we went to speak to a neighbor across the way. He told us that we had just missed the authorities.

"What do you mean, the authorities?" we all asked.

"That boy has been playing loud music at late hours of the night for months. Screams, bangs, barking, you name it. We've all complained but he swears it isn't him. He finally went crazy out here in the daytime and we called the police to come get him," he explained.

The young man hadn't been a drug user and didn't seem erratic when we had spoken or met the many times before. He claimed his paranormal activity, which was growing scarier by the night, happened late in the evening. He also had been quite alarmed when he called us just an hour ago, because he found his second dog dead in the home with no evidence to how it happened. He was frantic, and rightfully so, but not crazy. I had worked as a psychiatric technician for nearly four years in the state mental hospital … I knew crazy.

I stared at the house and wondered if something was glaring back at me, if my "attachment" had called me here to this house to be finished off somehow. I gladly got back in my friend's car and drove home. I thought long and hard at why this case had come to my attention and what had happened with the young man. We never got word of the young man again or his haunted house, but my car had not survived the case. That month in particular I had one car broken into and the other blown up, two terrifying paranormal cases with little conclusion, and more than nineteen random messages sent to me from psychics about my unwanted visitor and his presence in my life. However, I continued to ignore it.

Negative Energy?

How many coincidences make a fact? I often ask my clients this to validate the many signs we have in our lives that something divine is happening right before our eyes. I refused to believe I was experiencing something negative or paranormal, because I wanted to believe I was protected. I said my prayers, sprinkled my salt, grew up in a haunted house, and carried my totems; I was a good person. The fact still remains that the year concluded in a terrible divorce that left nothing but heartache, short sales on a beautiful home, damaged friendships, and regretful actions in its wake. In a desperate measure to find peace, I packed up what I could fit into my car and drove three states north to a new home in Minneapolis to start fresh. During my first week in the state of ten thousand lakes, I found a job at a spiritual event.

That's where a woman I had not met, never heard of, and did not know approached me as I was breaking down my booth at the fair. "Excuse me. I'd like to ask you if you'd care to have a free session with me. Your friend Dave said you could use it."

She seemed soft, friendly, and if my dear friend had referred her, who was I to turn down a free service of some kind. She was a shamanistic cord cutter and as she began to breathe in and out, swirling her sage smoke around me, she stopped and spoke softly in my ear. "Your sickness, your loss, your broken heart, your ovarian issues, and your unwanted visitor are all going to be healed. Just let go."

I wanted to stop her and ask what she was talking about. I wanted her to detail for me exactly what she meant. Instead I just followed her direction and truly accepted my own advice—how many coincidences make a fact. Something was "off" in my life and had been ever since that voice spoke to me in the hospital and, for whatever reason, I couldn't shake it. I had to let go of my ego, my underlying skepticism of the paranormal world I religiously announced existed, and have faith that the hokey psychic cleansing was going to work and that this woman was going to help me let go of it all.

I let go.

After a forty-five-minute "cord cutting" session, she finally directed me to open my eyes. I felt better somehow. I didn't see any lights or feel any divine presence, but I did feel better. In the months that followed this event I stopped having "bad luck," and I also stopped getting random messages from people to tell me I had something evil lurking around me. I didn't feel paranoid, I didn't feel pessimistic, and I had hope that something had been released from me.

Whether there is any truth to my negative attachment or not, I truly believe something followed me home from the hospital that night, and whatever it was, it knew me and how to bring darkness into my life.

I haven't changed my habits or routines in regard to the paranormal since this case, but instead have changed my faith. I believe wholeheartedly that we are always open to being a victim of negative energy. Like I said, I was a good person. I said my prayers, kept my crystals in my pocket, meditated and grounded before each case, and even kept an impeccable diet and exercise regiment to help ward off sickness. I tried to reduce stress, increase love, and focus, and yet still I have to be consciously aware that sometimes we don't choose to have an attachment but that they choose us.

When you look into the abyss, the abyss absolutely looks back…and sometimes comes home with you.

TEN

The White Noise Creatures

Working as a parapsychologist means I have to remain skeptical, but I'm aware that my passion started from a deep-rooted faith that something lives on beyond the physical death of the body. Parapsychology researches psychic phenomenon, conscious energy outside the human body, and strange occurrences that aren't otherwise empirically explained, and many paranormal concepts weave their way into my personal hauntings and research.

One such concept is that of Gestalt psychology and how the human brain processes and organizes sensory information. Objectively, as researchers, we try to measure and assess the health of our vision, our processing, the environment around us, and then question what we are seeing, hearing, or experiencing through philosophy and experimentation. Electronic voice phenomenon (EVP) within the paranormal realm is a common ground for philosophy, religion, and science to meld.

As a young girl, I remember being my own DJ and recording my voice over the commercials on the radio to introduce my favorite bands. Before CDs and MP3s, there were simple cassette tapes and record players; very easy to record and play with. I would play back my own personal narrated show and see if my parents would notice when going to listen to their favorite cassette. Possibly I was driven by that young ego shining through that wants nothing more than to hear their own voice, or the subconscious interest that radio frequency was this superpower; how does it all even work anyway? I found it fascinating that I could speak into a microphone and somehow, my words (these imaginary tidbits of data) were being recorded into history and played back again in the future.

Music, recording, and any auditory stimulus all seemed quite mystical to me. I must have had two or three shoeboxes full of those audiotapes I had recorded as a child. My mom even encouraged it. My sister and I both had collections of top-forty and holiday-themed tapes as us being the star disc jockeys.

You see, I had many strange experiences with white noise and electronic voice phenomenon, but I never associated it with the paranormal until I began doing parapsychological research nearly two decades later. My sister and I used to compare tapes as children, a spiritual competition so to speak, of who could get more ghost guests on their playback. Oddly, the playbacks never included the voice of the old woman that

we knew haunted our home. Instead, the voices were typically low-frequency male spirits. A low grumbling behind the
voices, behind the music…like they were having their own
conversation with us. Of course, you can't definitively choose a
gender, age, or any other quantitative trait to a frequency wave,
or voice, but they seemed to be alive.

That's the thing about playbacks, you hear this voice and it
is so different than the now common technology narrator. The
playbacks didn't sound like a computer. They didn't sound like
another band was being picked up or a strange coincidence of
random stations on scan. In the early '80s, cell phones and all
of the other frequency pollution was not nearly as common.
But the playbacks were always on our tapes and always seemed
to be very mindful and present. They were our ghost guests.

EVPs

For those who have never experienced electronic voice phenomenon, in my opinion it is one of the most compelling and
fascinating gateways into a possible spiritual realm. Many
skeptics would suggest the voices you hear within white noise
or on the playback of an audio segment are simply interference, synchronicity, or pareidolia. Interference could be from
any array of nearby electronic devices: from microwaves to
your neighbor's cell phone. Synchronicity could just be the
off chance you believe you're hearing something because you
are purposely there trying to get voices on your audio. This
want, this need, this power of suggestion also plays into the
psychological concept of pareidolia; that our mind will make

something out of otherwise random information. Like seeing rabbits in the clouds or faces in the wood on your door... so we hear voices on our tape recorders. For this reason, I have to clarify that my experiences have reached beyond the subtle and inconsistent voices that might be heard on an audio clip.

I'm not talking about the mumble or whisper lost within static that many people might interpret differently. I'm not talking about the audio clip you might see on your favorite paranormal TV show that requires a subtitle to understand... I'm talking about a voice. A crisp, clear voice. Voices that introduced themselves, had a name, and almost became our cohost to the program we were recording.

It was never something that was scary to me, because I had grown up with it. My dad was also very mechanical, and had often worked frequently on setting up my mother's physical equipment for her musical shows. My mother was a professional singer and recorded many things at home, so beyond-competent knowledge and equipment was an everyday occurrence in our house. It was very common to have interference, to have feedback, but these voices that my sister and I would record seemed to have a purpose.

The voices had a personality. It wasn't a detached English accent directing me down the street like a GPS, but instead was a unique voice all its own that always spoke about something relevant. If I was playing with Cow-Cow, my beloved stuffed animal and cohost, as a young girl, the voice might say, "Look at Cow-Cow wave." If I introduced my favorite band or song, the voices would applaud and say something positive like, "goodie." They weren't fearful or scary and were never demanding, but they were always present in those tapes. That's the thing about EVPs (electronic voice phenomenon), we as a paranormal field still are undetermined on what the voices are. Is this spirit communication, feedback, interference, or even projection of one's subconscious? We simply do not know for sure and without a definitive answer, the mind can run amuck.

From Beyond the Grave and Attic

When I was a teenager, there seemed to be a long stretch of time that I no longer received the voices. Looking back now, I suppose it was the fact cassette tapes moved to discs, which were much harder to record at home. I did receive EVPs on paranormal investigations that were done with my small handheld recorder cassette tape, but the voices at home were silenced by the inability to find a medium. My late-night talk shows with Cow-Cow were in the past, and so seemed the regular spirit voices. As a paranormal investigator, and a young woman who frequently shared her living quarters with guests from the other side, I did continue to get audibles— audio anomalies heard in real time without any type of tool or device. Quite frankly, the whispers continued throughout my life and still do, but my cohosted and narrated DJ shows were lost in my childhood. Until I found the shoebox.

I had finally cleaned out the storage unit in my father's upper garage that had been acquiring dust for nearly fifteen years. The relationship with my mother had grown extremely negative and distant, and my childhood was mocking me as I had acquired new responsibilities I wasn't yet mature enough to appreciate. I hadn't quite established a home for myself, but still felt the need to explore these boxes that had been forgotten about for so long. I nearly cried laughing when I realized after finding the shoebox full of cassette tapes that I would struggle to find a cassette player to enjoy them. Automobiles came standard with the disc player by then, and my last few cassette players had found new homes after a garage sale many years earlier.

Luckily, my dad had an old Ford Bronco with a cassette player still installed in the dash, so I found a spot in the driver's seat and spent the afternoon listening to my childhood adventures. Amazing '80s hair bands, a young capricious Sarah…and the voices. Plain as day two or three men could be heard talking in the background. Like a distant conversation a few feet behind my shoulder, men that were not with me in my bedroom, they had recorded their messages and legacy onto my cassette tape.

It was then I pieced the two experiences together. All of my childhood I had been experiencing the phenomena of electronic voices but didn't realize its importance to the paranormal puzzle until I was much older and had become a seasoned investigator. As a paranormal investigator, you hope to get a clear EVP so that no suggestion is needed when delivering the recording to a client. A type-A EVP is one that requires little-to-no audio cleanup or manipulation and typically is cognizant of the present conversation. If you have ever had the opportunity to gather an EVP with easy and instant playback that seems to be talking to you directly, you have hit the paranormal gold mine. Here I had a whole shoebox full of gold!

Of course, the home had long been remodeled and the voices were likely to have long been dissipated. I didn't have a cassette recorder on hand to try to reconnect, but I had lived in this house for more than a decade since its renovation. The voices didn't sound familiar and the energy seemed like a stranger to me. A quick rush of guilt moved over me to think someone had been trying to leave a message and it was an un-entertained child that was on the other end of the line the whole time. Then again, here I was getting their message all these years later with the opportunity to perhaps interject and bring peace. Who were these voices and did they belong to someone's loved one? Would anyone even be interested in these old, dusty tapes?

I do struggle with the concept of bringing peace to a spirit. After all, who am I to tell them to "cross over"? A part of me identifies with the late philosopher Friedrich Nietzsche; it seems so terribly selfish to interfere into the growing opportunity of a soul to die. Just as the concept of birth is monumental to a mother and child, I believe that death is also another vital growing experience and for us as living humans to hold hands with the spirit and guide them ... I feel that is selling a situation short. I wasn't sure if I should really listen to the messages and take them seriously. After all, what could they want from me?

White Noise Is the Background

There is no conclusion to this chapter in my life. I still get constant EVP activity on my Internet phone calls, my cellular phone calls, and on any type of data device I use to record during an investigation. I have experiences of audibles, actual real-time voices speaking in my apartment, but I usually disregard them. It has only been in the recent findings of science that I have found interest in all of the EVP activity that seems to haunt me. Why do some people have EVP all around them every time they record and others do not?

A dear friend I have known for more than a decade has created a theory with energy and sound that changes my whole belief system about an EVP. Some of his theory suggests intention has a very religious connotation; something that is hard for me to get on board with most times. However, if this man were not so brilliant—in my opinion genius—I might have passed up this math-heavy concept. Instead, I am back to being a learner and beginner in the art of the EVP and what it might really mean for our lives. Do these spirits mean what they say? Are these spirits communicating at all? Is pressing "record" meddling? Have I invited something just with an open ear?

Many paranormal researchers would absolutely agree that just as a Ouija board is a medium that invites spirits into your life, so is any other investigative tool; the recorder is no different. Definitively we don't know one way or the other if these voices belong to someone or something and what their intention is with intermingling in our lives. I do know that I have seen and heard some amazing evidence that requires me to include the use of EVPs in my paranormal research and spiritual journey. One such example happened a few years ago at an old abandoned hospital.

Mother, Is That You?

It was an old abandoned building once used as a hospital out in the middle of nowhere. Rumors circulated about the darkness around the land from Civil War to Native American hardships. Regardless of its history, I always had amazing paranormal experiences when staying overnight at this location. That particular evening, I was part of a small, intimate group of individuals investigating the emergency room. Though all the power had been turned off to the building, there was a particular location in the center of the room that would create high readings on the electromagnetic field detector. The Geiger counter (used to measure radiation) would spike, the tri-field meter (measuring magnetic, electric, and radio waves) would spike and no one knew exactly why. A handful of investigators sat in the middle of the room and had a real-time voice recorder that allotted for audio playback while in use. At first, it said nothing. But after a few moments, we began to hear static.

I took the role as narrator to ask clear and concise questions in hopes of getting a more accurate response. I asked everyone in the room to try to focus on grounding and to think of nothing (in hopes of reducing projection, though this is nearly impossible to do). The static became clearer. It was a voice speaking German. I explained to the voice coming through the recorder that I did not know German and would appreciate a conversation in English. It still spoke in German and continued to repeat the same thing. It then spoke out a name I did recognize, "Michael." I asked if anyone in the room was named Michael or had recently lost a loved one by that name. No one in the room seemed to have a connection. At that moment, four individuals walking by the room through the hospital halls entered in on our investigation. It was a man, a young woman, the young woman's friend, and a young boy. Though typically I agree that individuals should be much older if they are doing a paranormal investigation, the boy was only nine years old and was accompanied by his father. We welcomed them into the room and gave them a briefing about what was happening.

I laughed at the ordeal and explained to the new investigators that we were having a conversation in German, though none of us understood the language. One of the young ladies piped up that she had taken German in high school. We could not believe our luck and were so excited to have some possible answers on what this voice kept repeating!

Sure enough, when we called out in the room for something to convey its message again, it spoke out to Michael in the same German phrase. The young lady pieced together something about a car accident and a son. Immediately, just as the phrase had left her lips, the young boy in the room started to cry. He called out, "Mama, mama! Is that you?" The grown man scooped up his child and they quickly left the room. The boy was clawing at his dad's shoulders to be put down and come back to join us. His emotional response gave us all quite a chill. We finished up the EVP session and went back to our safe room and the kitchen area of the hospital.

Under bright lights and the safety of everyone gathered together, the conversation was discussed among the investigators. The father shortly entered the room and apologized for what had happened. His son Michael had just recently lost his mother. They had driven about forty-five miles to come to this small paranormal event in hopes of hearing from his mom. The little boy loved to watch the paranormal TV shows and thought his mom might come through. Neither the husband nor the son were prepared to hear a voice speaking in German directly to Michael. Michael's mom spoke German, visited Germany often, but had recently been killed in a car accident just miles from their home. The voice coming through the EVP seemed to know who would enter the room moments later ... and its message was received.

I have heard countless EVPs from the investigations of historical monuments, hospitals, and even cemeteries. The most meaningful, however, are those meant just for us. I do believe that something is trying to make a connection, and although I do not pretend to always know the intentions, I will never forget the tears from that young boy hearing a message from what he believed was his mother. I hope he finds peace that she is still with them. If indeed that was her at all.

ELEVEN

On the Road

Like most Midwest states, Iowa claims to have a bloody past in Native American genocide and therefore a heightened paranormal environment. Many small towns have brushed their violent history under the rug and continue to focus on the simple life at hand, but some Midwest towns are the opposite.

Between long stretches of highway and flat horizon there is the occasional town or city with no more than a small coffee shop and gas station. You stop in off the highway, away from the long stretch of highway in a town of four hundred, and get a cup of coffee. The waitress asks why you're out; you hesitate to mention a journey to a paranormal convention and then suddenly everyone in the café is as brimming as the coffee pot to share their local horror stories. Everyone has a story to tell if they know you might listen without judgment. Iowa is no different.

I had traveled from Kansas City nearly all night to reach my final destination alongside paranormal friends and colleagues in the city of Davenport, Iowa. Everyone had gathered in a hotel lobby to mingle and catch up on lost years and also to introduce themselves to people they had only known online up until this point. Some were fans of a local paranormal television show while others were interested in paranormal swag. I had come along because it was originally a party for a friend's birthday in combination with a paranormal conference. Some of my dear paranormal colleagues were going to be traveling to the remote city to celebrate and with only a five-hour drive over the border I couldn't resist.

Stephen was in the background. While everyone else was clinking their cups brimming with alcohol, Stephen sat in the dark corner of the room sipping whiskey and chugging a beer. He had a soft energy about him and a very mysterious demeanor. He wore dark clothing, seemed to always be tapping his foot to the tune playing in the background and was people-watching almost as much as I was. To know that he was the brother of my friend here at the party I was excited to introduce myself. I suppose we immediately hit it off. We have been close friends ever since. Even though his brother has long since left the picture, Stephen and I still keep in touch.

Stephen and I talked about music, about playing the guitar, and even about quantum mechanics and its relevance to the paranormal community. We talked engineering, we talked alcohol, and we even told dirty jokes, but one thing we didn't do was expend any negative energy or talk drama like the majority of the people present. That weekend was not spent partying or mingling, instead it was spent with late-hour lobby conversations and conversations at the diner with Stephen. My brain was on a high, and hearing Stephen talk about his theories was new and invigorating. We continued to talk on the phone occasionally and send a text from time to time, but I really wanted to have a few more conversations with Stephen in person after the event in Iowa had long since passed. He really had some amazing ideas. I decided to plan a road trip to visit Stephen in person though he lived many hours away.

At the time, Stephen was a musician playing in many different venues throughout the weekend, so between setting up his musical equipment and meeting his friends in the local bar scene, we also shared deep conversations about the Möbius loop and quantum mechanics. The conversations that Stephen I would share were so deeply meaningful that I instantly had an epiphany move over me and my perception for life, and at that moment things seemed to change forever. I suppose you could call it a philosophical high, an unforgettable moment, but to simply share this experience over beers and cigars on the front porch was a large key factor in the fact that our friendship has remained strong to this day. Stephen now has a book on many of his theories and continues to play shows from time to time. I continuously think about some of the theories that we discuss and also about the contents of his book and research. I ask you, the reader, to determine what it is you think haunts a location and why.

My relationship with the paranormal was beginning to grow into an almost complete philosophical and scientific category of my life. Religion, spirituality, and faith had all but left me and I knew there was something empirical to prove. I became obsessed with measurements, utilizing scientific theory, and gaining as much data as I could. I went from doing therapy and spiritual guidance work with clients to traveling the world and experiencing some of the most haunted locations on earth and taking quantitative measurements when I could. I created a computer program that helps to find a correlation and pattern and empirical data with each paranormal experience. I was obsessed in a completely detached way.

Then I got a call about a client one state to the east of where I live. This wasn't a client experiencing moving furniture or bumps in the night, but was a family that had agreed to undergo an exorcism with their only daughter. This was that exorcism that still remains sharply heart-wrenching in my memory today.

A Midwest Devil

The call came in the afternoon; the family had found me through a friend I worked with at a local cellular phone company. This coworker had overheard my adventures and knew of my paranormal expeditions, and when a girl from her Christian outreach group in her hometown started having strange occurrences, she recommended me to the family while home on holiday. It was a short two-hour drive to the east from where I lived at the time and though I had never experienced an exorcism before, I knew what an exorcism was; I had grown up a devout Southern Baptist.

Of course, most of us have seen the movie, perhaps we have a preconceived notion of what to expect; I even had memories from a favorite '80s parody movie that popped in my head and that was accompanied by my own laughter. The thought of an exorcism wasn't really all that scary to me. I was completing my undergraduate degree in psychology and forensics at the time and felt as though my experience in the paranormal and formal education could possibly help the family before and after the exorcism was to take place. I was also relieved to learn that a great friend of mine was working on the case and was to be the pastor performing the exorcism. This was particularly meaningful, because we didn't see each other often and only talked by phone monthly.

My hopes were to utilize my experience as a counselor to minimize stress and guide the family through this terribly emotional time in their lives.

I remember pulling up to the small town and wondering how something so huge could happen to a city so small. What was it about some demonic presence that found a home in this tiny, white, two-story farmhouse in the Midwest? To my dismay, I had learned the family had contacted many paranormal television shows to also capture the experience. They were so adamant in their faith they wanted to be sure and prove to those who had doubt just what was happening in their home and what had happened with their daughter.

I suppose they felt if the cable television show or national network was willing to air the experience that must stand for some large amount of validation. I, however, never felt quite right about having a slew of TV personnel present in such a scary and intimate experience. As the makeshift therapist involved, I quite frankly feared for the safety and well-being of the daughter.

At first I began to have great suspicions about the parents. Perhaps the parents had convinced the children to play along in this grand dramatic scheme so that they could make money, gain notoriety, or build some small mound of fame off the experience. The small town did have some history of bank robbers and booze runners during prohibition; perhaps it was the ghost of some gangster involved in their family drama. Nonetheless, I didn't have much luck getting the family to sit down in a quiet environment to talk about the stress in and around their lives.

I did, however, spend a few hours with the young girl before she was exorcised. The pastor who was going to be performing the services had asked me if I felt her experience was exacerbated by her family; we both agreed it had been. It was a very complicated case and I trusted the pastor to do what he felt was right. I vividly remember the girl being nearly unconscious though she was fit to be in her room without any medical intervention. She would go in and out of wakefulness, and at one point could have a very lucid conversation while at other times she was almost catatonic.

The day of the exorcism, she lay lifeless in her bed. She was breathing on her own, had a mild amount of perspiration, and maybe weighed a hundred pounds soaking wet. Her blond hair was stuck to her forehead and her bony figure was wrapped tightly in the blue sheets on her bed. She didn't respond when I asked questions and only really came to life at the presence of her mother when she visited her bedside with food and water. The young girl was quite the actress if this was all a scam. You could tell by her skin tone that perhaps she really was sick.

Wavering on whether or not the exorcism was a real situation, I talked with the pastor about his ability to perform the task. The religious authorities had apparently believed this to be a true situation of great spiritual relevance and had approved the process. The Vatican holds a special reverence for exorcisms. The drama on set was that a real exorcism is not to be filmed on camera, and there was much discussion about whether or not the filming could or should be done.

I remember the moments before the exorcism was to take place; I visited the daughter one last time to let her know what was going to happen. She still lay in the bed unconscious, looking very malnourished, and did not respond when I explained the likely stress she was to endure. Just as I left the room, I backed up against the corner of the door by her closet and watched her parents change her dressings. Again, at this time in my life my paranormal experiences were being filtered through a very heavy scientific perception. I was skeptical of almost everything and truly needed evidence to maintain some amount of spirituality, most of which was completely gone at this point in my life. Perhaps that was the divine timing of me working on this case.

Her mother lifted her onto her left side and her father, brother, and a member of the television crew reached underneath to change her nightgown. All four people were struggling to lift her body even a few inches off of the bed. This young girl who was half my size appeared so heavy that three adult people were shaking at the weight of just lifting half her body. I simply cocked my head to the side and with wide eyes continued to stare. What would normally be a quick five-minute process turned into a thirty-minute struggle. I couldn't believe it.

Before I crept completely out of the room, I reached back to touch the arm of the young woman. I touched her skin for the first time that day and she felt as though she was on fire. The texture of her skin was no longer soft or delicate and instead was hard as stone. My arm jerked back in fear; physics were defying me. The laws of nature were bending before my very eyes and I wasn't quite sure if I could accept it. Just as I went around the corner of the room, I looked back over my shoulder as the room emptied and the film crew readied themselves.

I leaned over to my friend the pastor, "What in the hell is going on here?"

He looked up at me, with his soft brown eyes, "It is beginning to ready itself. They always seem to know when we're here."

His response didn't completely make sense to me and I simply smiled as he walked into the young woman's room. I wished him luck and sat downstairs just off the main banister into the living room. The family had left down the hall alongside me and just as they closed the door at our leaving, things could be seen moving under the sheets of the young woman. It sounds absolutely crazy, even as I'm telling this to you now, but it's true. She lay as still and heavy in the bed as I had left her moments before and yet it looked as though wind was blowing underneath the blanket next to her body. Like a tail of a cat was swishing beneath the bed sheets. None of it made sense.

I had expected to see staff running out of the bedroom covered in green pea soup or even hear the bed thumping loudly through the floor during the exorcism. Instead, we didn't hear much at all. I heard the pastor reciting from his Bible, and I heard some declarations of faith, but no growls or screams as I had half-expected. Three and a half hours later, the pastor came down the front entryway stairs. He looked exhausted. He asked for an ice water as he needed to check his blood sugar, and I asked permission to visit the daughter and check on her now that the exorcism was complete.

Walking up the stairs seemed to happen in slow motion. I suppose I had false expectations again that perhaps a growl would meet me at the top of the stairs. I guess I thought I would come around the corner and open her door and see eyes glowing red and a levitating young woman. Instead, she lay there like she had a few days previous. She had more pink in her complexion but just as much perspiration over her brow. She still didn't respond to my questions, but before I left I had to know; I had to touch her. I walked back to her room, and touched her arm. Her skin felt normal to the touch. Once again it felt soft and delicate like the skin on my own arm, and I had to second guess what I had experienced just three hours before. Had that strange occurrence really happened? Had some simple passages from the Bible bent the world as I knew it back into place? What exactly had happened to us here in this little farmhouse? I wasn't sure.

Introspection

The truth is, that's the only exorcism I've ever been a part of. Because I'm not a member of the clergy I wasn't allowed to be in the room, but I was downstairs the whole time and I felt as though I was a part of this whole life-changing experience. I saw the client both before and after the exorcism and quite honestly didn't notice too much of a difference in her demeanor. I spoke with her a few days later after all the commotion had resolved and she seemed to have gained a level-headed consciousness, and she had little-to-no recollection of the experience or the drama that had taken place in her home. She had remembered one of the crew members only because she was a fan of his show. The whole thing blew over just as quickly as it had come into my life. That's it, it was over.

I occasionally get updates about the young woman from a coworker, but my expectations and assumptions of that day, as well as my conclusion to the experience, are still a little unnerving and incomplete. I actually have long hoped to talk with the pastor in person about that day and try to get an explanation to her hot, heavy skin, her excessive weight and excessive perspiration, and what had happened during the exorcism.

Sadly, I never got the chance as this pastor is no longer with us. His passion was always removing the stress from others, and perhaps he had never actually gotten rid of the stress…it had only moved into him and he had taken it on himself. Many people believe it was his overly kind heart that killed him in the end. Regardless, the world is less one great man, and I have an experience that may never find resolution.

TWELVE

The Patient
Never Left

Of all the haunted locations I have had the honor and pleasure of investigating, there are always a handful of locations that reign supreme. Some locations that host hauntings and ghost events are historical monuments that come with a special tour, guided commentary, and even old black-and-white photos in the gift shop of what used to be at the location. Saloons with gunfight residue still left on the walls, old railway stations that were the home of gangster shoot-outs, and even hospitals that brag about the number of patients who have died on the premises through an array of different disorders and diseases.

Some of the locations don't need a story; their history is all but completely overlooked by their grand architecture or wide-open spaces. Some old hospitals tell no tales, but instead you find yourself lost in the vines that overgrow stone and you feel mysteriously connected to all the patients who had ever lived there as you walk through the crumbling rooms one after the other. Some locations have little-to-no history but instead boast built legends and lore; they still have a grand monument or purpose that lures you in, such as a huge boiler or steam mill out in the middle of nowhere. Some locations are not haunted at all, but perhaps carry the adrenaline forever forward from the tourists that flock to a Hollywood hotspot of terror. A movie that might once have featured a home to a perhaps completely fictitious tale, but yet kept all the moviegoers sleepless in their beds and empty of their pockets.

My point is, some haunted locations are forgetable, and others you can't forget even if you try. Even just thinking about introducing this hospital reminds me of how heavy it lives within my subconscious. This was not the same haunted hospital that had a ghostly entity call out to me by name, but instead is a location nestled alone in the Midwest. It wasn't famous for its tuberculosis patients or death chutes but grew famous by the whispers and tales of those who visited. This hospital is not only a location with excessive paranormal activity but also has a gruesome history. Experiencing the medical facility long forgotten by its previous owners is a horrifying experience. My first visit to this hospital meant the staff and I camped out in dilapidated patient rooms with gaping holes in the walls representing old window shafts, and bugs kept us company in the night; there was no electricity or running water, and more than a few things that went bump in the night.

During the day I found myself exploring the hallways and digging through old patient files; quite a nightmare for today's modern medical privacy act. It was as if one day the staff and patients just walked out of the building and left everything right where it was. Aside from the ceiling crumbling onto the floor, the heavy mold in the basement, and the outdated machines, it was all real. The environment now looked like a successful dystopic Hollywood production with the cast and crew gone for lunch. The unique and refreshing paranormal experience at this haunted hospital location was that the hall-ways could be bustling with event staff and the sun could be high in the sky... and activity still continued.

Chairs would move, people would be pushed and scratched, and you would swear the place was crawling with rodents the way black figures moved in the lower corners of your eyes. Doors would slam in our faces, our equipment would stop working and malfunction more times than could be counted, and it wasn't even worth keeping extra batteries on-site because they were all dead within an hour, even while still in their plastic containers. Going into the location as a very skeptical researcher, I was astounded at the range of activity—from electronic voice phenomenon to real apparitions—that seemed to happen around every corner.

As I mentioned, during my first visit to the hospital I found the location quite dilapidated. It had not been kept up and it was a local paranormal team that had undertaken the respon-sibility of revitalizing it. Quite honestly, knowing what I know

now, it should've been condemned. The mold and open pipes alone should have deterred anyone from staying. My week stay at the haunted hospital included an array of paranormal experiences, however, and for that reason, we all kept coming back.

At first, we assumed the evidence gathered in the daytime was likely somebody else moving around the location. Anytime we heard a bump, bang, or the slam of a door it could be justified with the thought that someone was likely down the hall. It wasn't until later in the afternoon that we would catch up with staff around the bonfire and discuss when and where we were throughout the day. It was then I began to ask who had been going in and out of the rooms on the first floor just an hour ago. There had been footsteps, voices, even the slamming of doors more than four or five times. But I discovered that I had been alone in the hospital. Unconsciously, I tried to rationalize maybe it was the wind. But a large part of me wondered how many coincidences make a fact, and how long do I remain skeptical when it's likely that something could be going on?

I was excited to pay more attention the next day. I knew if I heard a noise then I would have to investigate it and make sure every single circumstance could be rationalized before I jumped to any paranormal conclusions. There I was, on the second floor in the patient room at the end of the hall, which was noted to be very haunted indeed, and I sat quietly by myself on the floor. After about forty-five minutes of little-to-no activity, I gathered my things and began to walk out the door. It was then that the cupboard in the corner of the room slammed behind me. I hadn't seen anything and it was just a loud noise, so I slowly turned around and watched the room. There were no open vents, working central air, or even any open windows in this room. I hadn't gotten up quickly enough to make much noise and the cupboard seemed to slam close with a large amount of vigor.

I could feel my heart racing and my blood pumping harder throughout my veins. I clenched my fists and took a deep breath. I noted the details of the room. I made sure my inner narrative was slow and calm, and I began to get control over my vitals once again. I always criticized ghost hunters or paranormal investigators for responding in fear. It's important to get control of your central nervous system and avoid the fight-or-flight response and just be calm.

"Who's there?" I asked.

I waited for a response; thinking for sure after the largely slammed cabinet that I would have someone willing to speak, but nothing. I began to laugh under my breath at the thought I wasn't alone in this room after all and maybe I did have a willing participant. It was exciting, scary, and fun. I readjusted my backpack around my shoulder and turned around, leaving my back open to the corner of the room I had just been speaking to. It was a barren patient room. It was three o'clock in the afternoon, the sun was shining brightly, I was alone on the second floor, and here I was talking to an empty corner. I huffed with disbelief; I had almost become one of those over-exaggerated investigators.

Just then I was grabbed tightly from behind and thrown backward onto the hard floor. It was much more than a nudge. Now, I will be the first to admit that I probably trip over nothing more often than the average person. I fall up stairs more than I do down, I have nearly cut my fingers off cooking a handful of times, but this was not a trip over nothing: Someone had grabbed me. It reminded me of the days in middle school when I'd be all secure in my book bag straps, walking nonchalantly down the hall when just then a good friend would run up behind me and grab the upper part of my book bag, pulling my shoulders down as I tried to carry their weight. I had been so unsuspecting that the whole of my bag dropped my body weight to the ground. I sat on the floor in shock. A large part of me wanted to quickly get up and run the hell away from this part of the hospital. I don't always know what we think we're running from when we start from a paranormal experience, as if the ghost couldn't follow us anywhere and possibly travel through time, but nonetheless I wanted to escape. However, I just sat; I was quite honestly too terrified to move or turn around. I just sat wide-opened and in shock.

Mostly I was scared of the pre-suggestive stories I had heard around the bonfire the night before about this particular part of the hospital. It was rumored that an older woman was a patient in this room and had been abused by the hospital staff. It was said that she was a very lively and violent patient that possibly was experiencing some level of delusion or mental health trauma. I couldn't help but recollect my days working in the state mental health hospital when mentally ill offenders would change their behavior at the drop of a hat. We were taught never to turn our back to a patient and to always be prepared.

Here I was, unprepared, my back to whatever it was in this patient room, and sitting on the floor completely vulnerable. Suddenly the sun in the room and the brightness of my surroundings didn't matter at all; I was scared. I waited for something to grab me from behind again and drag me into that corner of the room; something scary from a dark horror movie that might drag me up the wall and have me dangling in horror from the ceiling. I don't know what I expected of a violent spirit, but that's quite possibly the scariest thing of all.

I sat like a young toddler alone on the floor with my hands covering my eyes, pretending if whatever I couldn't see wasn't there, maybe it would leave me alone. The adrenaline passed, my heartbeat slowed down, and time ticked on. I gently shifted my weight onto my right hip and looked over my right shoulder back into the room. Again, I saw nothing. This time I did laugh under my breath and I quietly said, "Thank you for letting me visit," as I hastened my steps back down the hallway to the staircase. I skipped down the hall and gravitated toward the front of the hospital where everyone seemed to gather throughout the day to smoke their cigarettes and swap stories. They could tell something had just happened. One of the two younger gentlemen hunched over the bonfire asked me one simple question, "Where were you?"

"The second floor," I responded. "That um ... room at the end of the hall."

"What did she do? Did she scream at you?" Both of the boys didn't look surprised and instead were intrigued.

"No, no…" I exclaimed as I relaxed with my hands now over my knees as I sat gently down on the bench against the wall. "Just some loud noises, and then she grabbed me."

The two boys kind of laughed and one inhaled deeply on his cigarette. The crackling ember at the end of his cigarette hissed as his other friend cackled over my reaction.

"She'll get ya; that bitch will get you," he laughed.

I guess my experience wasn't all that interesting, and in fact perhaps was a little too subtle for their taste and experience at the old hospital. Perhaps the woman had liked me, because from the stories I heard throughout the night, she clearly was not very shy at letting her presence be known. That very evening it seemed as though my mental perceptions had changed a bit. As the sun went down, I felt less secure in my skin; I didn't feel like a skeptic entering into a historical hospital with the possibility that something "might" happen. Instead, I felt like a victim walking blindly into a situation I was vaguely prepared for that felt unsafe. It reminded me of that time as a child hiding under my covers from some evil thing looming in the hall. I didn't have the sanctuary of my old home, my warm covers, or my family just across the hall. However, as a grown woman who had experienced many paranormal occurrences, I knew I could handle myself up to this point.

Never had I been in such a paranormal hotspot with such a high level of activity. It was invigorating.

Lovely Lullaby

It was that very night I had a run-in with the entity in the basement. I tried to avoid the stories and myths of the alleged spirits in the hospital so I could keep a clear mind. I didn't want any of my evidence to be polluted with some personal bias or by the power of suggestion. I truly hoped to capture evidence and nothing more. I always try to come at investigating with an objective point of view and not have a story lingering in the back of my mind that I hoped would fit the evidence.

Unfortunately, the staff at this location and the many people who visit it frequently can't help but share their stories, and also share their opinions. I was told walking into the basement could be a very dangerous thing to do, especially at night. People had reported being scratched, having large objects thrown at them, very violent noises and screams, and the history seemed to suggest the hospital basement is where the spirits spent most of their time, and they did not want to be interrupted. Aside from the paranormal phenomenon said to happen in the basement, it was also littered with broken pipes and crumbling structures.

I held my flashlight with a sense of security, though I was grasping tightly onto the shirt of the person in front of me as we walked down the stairs to the hotspot in the basement. A good friend and staff member was giving me a tour of the basement just before sundown that evening. The floor had open plumbing and sharp pipes were jutting out from the beams in the ceiling. The basement of the hospital was half underground and therefore it let little natural light into the room with lots of shadow play on the walls.

There was this strange yellowish-green hue in the room as the light fought to shine through the badly stained glass covered with dirt. It seemed as though the basement served as a meeting room for doctors, headquarters for maintenance and janitorial services, and also was the location of the cafeteria and other casual workings of a modern hospital. The environment itself was unfriendly. I had to walk through cobwebs, over rusty nails and dilapidated equipment, and walk from room to room through tight spaces with little light. The rumors of the violent spirits roaming these halls didn't help my nerves either.

My friend and I went into an old dark laundry room adjacent to a closet and found a quiet place on the floor to sweep off the dust, sit quietly, and perhaps collect some evidence. I particularly liked the staff member because of his professionalism and his kind energy. I figured with two respectable adults minding their own business and remaining objective, simply sitting still and alone, we would perhaps gather some friendly evidence to deter the horrible stories we had heard up to this point.

We sat on the floor just long enough for the sun to go down and for the shadows to crawl across the floor and escape completely out of the cold basement. We were left in the dark with the small amount of illumination our glow stick provided and we quietly discussed which pieces of equipment we should use. As we kept our conversation to a minimum I couldn't help but hear something in my mind's eye; like a low voice in the back of my mind bothering me to come forward.

I had done my spiritual protection ritual that I do before most every investigation and even had my lucky quartz in my pocket. Surely, this evil, dark spirit in the basement wasn't creeping inside my inner thoughts. I had specifically asked myself to refrain from any psychic work and to ignore any and all psychic messages I might get from the location, so I tried to just push through and ignore it. My research at that time was on binaural beats, which are tones and frequencies used to alter state of consciousness. Some cultures believe binaural beats and lucid dreaming, meditation, out-of-body experiences, and self-healing are all closely related. For some, when they use binaural beats, they can "see" things that are not otherwise there. I wanted any investigations to remain as objective as possible; no psychic stuff. However, sitting here in the dark in this room…something popped into my head that I just couldn't ignore. I felt talking about the subject would bring about unhappy feelings from my investigative partner, so again, I just tried to push the voice as far from my mind as it would go. Psychically, I just knew that the comment and song repeating in my head would be hurtful to my partner; that was the intent all along. I knew this wasn't my own thought, and the longer I sat there the less control I had at keeping it to myself.

So I apologized ahead of time, "I'm so sorry for what I have to say," I murmured. "I truly feel as though this popped into my head about five minutes ago and since then the energy in this room has changed. I don't know where this is coming from, but I have to say it."

My partner insisted I go ahead and let it out if I needed to, and though I was sure it would not be positive, I let the lullaby drain from my thoughts. I began to hum a childhood tune, and as if I were acting in a theater production, my delivery changed. I felt the need to hunch over and lower my eyebrows, to lower my voice and to say my phrase with a cocked grin upon my face. Even though we were sitting in the dark, and the delivery likely would be unnoticed, I felt obligated nonetheless.

"Gimme your best shot little boy." I hissed after humming my tune.

I could hear my partner gasp with surprise. Without hesitation my fellow investigator looked at me—looked through me—"Really? That's what you have to say to me?" He wasn't talking to me, but instead that short phrase had triggered a connection to some unfinished experience in his life.

The lullaby that I sang and the phrase that I coughed at him had made complete sense. He knew the spirit was trying to muster up old unfinished business and indeed it had. After I had said it, I immediately felt better. I felt like I had my body back and that my mind was once again my own.

"I'm so sorry, I just had to say that. It just kept repeating in my mind over and over and over. What did that mean to you?" I reached out as I asked.

"Nothing. Nothing I really want to talk about while we're down here."

I could respect that. That's one of those gray areas that I struggle with as a forensic psychologist but also as a parapsychology researcher. A large part of me desperately wants to know the innermost fears of a person and how that might be brought out in a paranormal experience. However, I also empathize on a very deep level about what that fear is like when you are completely vulnerable and alone in the dark and something taps at your soul. My curiosity wanted to know what message I had received and why. However, I also had to respect the wisdom of my fellow investigator and respect his wishes to keep his guard up and his intimate life situations at bay.

We gathered up our equipment, and decided to move into another room. Perhaps a change of scenery would give us a change of energy too. We sat in the large open room adjacent to the hallway that would lead us upstairs if we had to make a quick getaway. We knew if we grew tired or exhausted we could simply escape with a quick exit if we were in this main area. We also had an idea that if this entity was to continue to follow us into the next room and ventured to become violent, we could move with haste to the most convenient exit and safety.

We decided not to unpack all of our equipment as we had done in the room before and just gathered the essentials out around us. Instead, we simply sat quietly in the room and waited to see if anything happened. We didn't ask any open-ended questions into the dark and we also didn't instigate any malevolent rebuttals. We simply sat quietly with our backs against each other to get a sense of the environment.

After a long dark silence, the kind long enough to make you question your own sanity, we began to hear rustling in the corner of the room. We knew quite well it could be a rat or rodent, but that was not the scariest explanation. I asked loudly to my partner, "Did you hear that?"

"Yes, from over there on your left at about one hundred feet." He answered me quickly and with a confident authority to his voice.

It was exactly where I had heard the noise as well and despite the fact I was facing in that direction with little-to-no distractions, I hadn't seen anything at all with my eyes.

"Probably the roof falling in on us," I laughed out loud. Just as my partner began to laugh along with me, the energy and mood was quickly interrupted with a strong yank of my hair.

"Ouch! What the hell!" The yank came so hard that my partner had felt it as well. We both jerked in reaction. By the time the exclamation left my lips, my fellow investigator was on his feet suggesting that we quickly move along and head upstairs. I completely trusted the person I was with that night and therefore knew it wasn't him pulling my hair just to get a laugh out of me. We gathered our things and without hesitation booked it toward the hall at the end of the room.

I have thought about the scenario many times in my mind, and quite honestly I don't even think he could've pulled my hair as it was wound tightly in an upper bun. He was holding his equipment as was I and we both sat back to back; I hadn't felt him move and only felt his breathing before the yank happened.

We made our exit to the staircase and quickly jolted down the long, slender hallway back to the open patio area in front of the hospital. We wiped the sweat from our brow and looked at each other for a moment. What had we just experienced? We knew all the tales of people getting hit over the head and things thrown at them, but we weren't entirely sure if they were true. He had investigated this location long enough to know what was real and what wasn't, and even though it may not have had a logical explanation his intuition of when to safely leave a location before things got too bad was always very accurate. Neither he nor I had any definitive conclusions to what happened that night in the basement.

After the recovery of my hair being yanked I even forgot to ask him about the phrase I had whispered to him nearly an hour before the incident occurred. What I do remember is the emotional stress that we shared that night. Perhaps that's the scariest thing about this location. Not only do strange things happen in strange places, and noises and bangs continue throughout the day and night, but you begin to question your safety. From sunup to sundown and from room to room you're constantly on guard wondering what's going to happen next. Scarier still is perhaps the emotional stress that the hospital puts upon its visitors when they enter and long after they leave as well.

For those who have visited this location, regardless of how many times, or who have worked as a part of the volunteer staff at this haunted hospital, it's hard to deny the irritability one picks up while staying at this location. Oftentimes couples will be fighting, best friends will be in a quarrel, and staff members that shared a hospitable lunch just moments prior will hatefully fight over equipment once they return to the haunted halls. It is as if we become a pawn in some game for the spirits; entertainment in the living.

I have been to this hospital four times now and each and every experience is unique. Each and every visit I have I lose a number of things from my luggage, and typically find myself in a bad mood more than a handful of times while visiting. For no reason at all, I will simply feel frustrated and anxious.

Despite the great company and historical location, and the plethora of evidence one walks away with upon visiting this haunted hospital, you have to be emotionally and spiritually prepared while present at this location and even after you leave.

I truly believe in energy and the laws of physics; that energy does not die but instead transfers. I believe sometimes we come home from the haunted locations with intentions on making a connection, and though we may not consciously realize it, we have; and it transfers its way into our lives and away from the crumbling structure it haunts. It haunts you long after you leave.

In this case, the hospital still lingers in my dreams and calls to me for a visit again soon.

THIRTEEN

The Little Cemetery at the Top of a Hill

I oftentimes brag that my sister is responsible for much of my paranormal enthusiasm. As I mentioned before, from a young age she was always guiding me through homemade haunted houses, reading me scary tales at night, and making sure to put on Freddy Krueger's *A Nightmare on Elm Street* the moment Mom and Dad's car faded into the end of the driveway.

When we both grew much older, my sister and I joined a paranormal research group out of Kansas City, Missouri. It was a long-established group of metaphysical individuals who taught workshops, lectures, and took residential cases quite seriously. Serious enough, in fact, that I was not allowed to investigate as a part of the team until I had shadowed them for at least a year. Though my sister went to college away from home, we would each attend the psychic fairs, the workshops, and, when we had the chance, do investigations of our own. My sister's psychic ability ranges from animal communication to psychometry (the ability to "read" an object by touch). She typically gets visual cues and messages whereas I get audio evidence and voices. I tend to empathize with life trauma and connect with loved ones who have crossed over whereas my sister connects with animals and objects more frequently. Together we are a great psychic team.

One summer she was home from college and we were both exploring the history of our town in search of a new paranormal hotspot to practice our talents. She had heard from a coworker at her summer job that an area just a few miles up the road was terribly haunted. It was a short drive so we decided to pack up and head out on a warm spring evening.

My sister and I both well know that when people get a hint that you're interested in the paranormal they immediately share their haunted tales with you. What would otherwise be a very intimate and taboo subject quickly becomes a feverishly exciting story. Some people want to share the dust-particle images on their photos whereas others request dream interpretation. We didn't take haunted stories very seriously anymore because they were a dime a dozen and most seemed to be a summary of a popular scary legend or story. The reason my sister had asked me to look at this location in particular was because this was the first time the scary stories had come to us. We hadn't prompted it at all and it seemed honest. I had a teacher at school who also shared a terrifying experience at this location, similar to one of my sister's old friends; it screamed to be investigated.

We decided to prepare for a weekend investigation of this haunted hotspot and couldn't wait to explore the mysteries behind the stories we were hearing. We gathered our flashlights and extra batteries, made sure our first aid kit was fully stocked, and then tucked a hand recording device in each pocket and a tablet of paper for notes. Though we had all sorts of technological equipment to investigate with, my sister and I have both found it's best to sometimes just bring ourselves in a healthy state of mind with a tablet of paper and pens. Electrical devices can fail, batteries go dead, and at the very least we can dictate our evidence or experience the moment it happens.

Our destination was about six miles up the road from where we lived. The area had long since been very active Native American heartland that underwent commercial construction. There was a golf course, an airport, some residential neighborhoods, and still some barren stretches of land connecting one road to the other. At night, after business hours, it was still quite dark and desolate. The story went that the land itself was haunted; which isn't such a stretch of the mind considering Missouri's history of the Civil War, slavery, slaughtering of the Indians, and so forth. However, it was also said that the building of the condominiums and the airport was done around a small stretch of land that housed a private cemetery; a small, untouched and undisturbed piece of history. It was unsure who was buried in the cemetery, but it was a fifty- to sixty-person lot and was dwarfed by the airport at the edge of the property. There were no gates, no signs, and most of the tombstones were so old and decrepit they were unable to be deciphered. This location couldn't be found using a GPS, and we actually had to do some digging to determine just where this hotspot was located. We decided on the way we would also stop at a few other legendary paranormal venues: a Super 8 motel, a burial ground, and an old slave trade location. Our journey, of course, started out by driving down one particular street.

We drove down Spooky Street, likely holding our breath, but reached the end of the road with no gruesome obstacles. Perhaps a funny feeling or some butterflies in the stomach, but nothing jumped out and began the evening with the definitive apparition. We pulled into the gas station to make sure our tank was full and also to grab a few ice waters. I believe I grabbed some beef jerky and cheese as well, and some extra batteries just in case. Upon checkout, we mentioned to the clerk where we were going and asked if he had heard any stories. He laughed that his stories were much stranger, but were of some Friday night customers and not ghosts. We gathered our goods and moved back to the car, then drove off into the distance toward the small cemetery on a hill.

I was pretty sure I knew where this location was, considering that many of my high school peers had partied at a chunk of land just up the road from the airport. I had remembered being at one of these bonfires and sitting on the tailgate, counting airplanes going up overhead. The location was also near some soccer fields where I used to coach cheerleading, and I remembered getting lost my very first time there and being late to the first meeting as coach. It seemed destiny had brought me to the brim of this hotspot many times. It was embarrassing, but I do remember the winding roads and the short turns just beyond the airport on the horizon. I was a little nervous we would be driving the stretch in the pitch dark, however, that's typically the best time to investigate; when the rest of the world is a little quieter against the darkness.

On the way there, we took a road that would drive us past the house of an old friend. I had briefly dated this young man in grade school and knew his family quite well. He had been a friend for a few years and our senior year of high school he had been hit by a drunk driver and died. Though the flowers and teddy bears were nailed to a cross halfway across town, I believed his family still lived in this home in the backwoods of our neighborhood.

I slowed the car down and thought about him as we approached. I could see the outline of the house on the horizon and remembered pulling up to it time and time again in my past. My sister had commented on why I was slowing down; she thought that perhaps maybe I had seen a deer. As she looked at me in the dim of my dashboard lights she could tell there was more to my slowed pace. "Do you know someone who lives here?" she asked.

I didn't answer right away. I smiled under my breath and looked over at her, "I know someone who used to live here. He died a few years ago. You remember Eugene?" Just as she nodded her head in agreement that she indeed remembered the young man, she jerked her hands out in front of her body as if to prepare for an accident or head-on collision.

"Look out!" she screamed.

I turned my attention back to the road we were driving on and did see something crossing into my headlights. I slammed on the brakes and prayed I would not hear or feel a sudden stop. My eyes were still closed when a heavy feeling moved over my body. It was at that moment that my sister reached out and clenched my upper thigh just over the stick shift. My eyes rolled down to my lower right, followed her arm up, and I looked past her shoulders and into her eyes: There was fear. I didn't see my sister scared very often. In fact, I think I could count just a few times my sister was ever truly scared, but this was making its way to the top of that list. Her reaction, mixed with my intuition, made me lock eyes with her, because I, too, did not want to see what had created such a spook in my sibling. I mouthed to her quietly, "What is it?" Even then I had unconsciously used the word "it" and did not assign a gender to what was loitering ahead in my high beams.

"Look," she whispered. I slowly turned my head back over my left shoulder and out over the hood of my car. There it stood: A shadow of something straight ahead, no more than twenty feet in front of my vehicle. I sat there in idle, waiting for it to cross the street. Unconsciously, I believe there was fear, because it was the shadow of something that didn't exist. The shadow was in the shape of a tall, slender man. I couldn't see clothing, shoes, a hat, or any dangerous props, but instead the long and lengthy figure of a man staring at us. It didn't have eyes, it didn't have a face, but it was staring at us. It was almost as if I was trying to communicate with

Eugene and had mentally put my place in the spiritual world to connect, and instead crossed paths with this "thing."

It was frozen in time, and just as I began to speak, the words halted at my lips. The long slender figure, a silhouetted shadow refusing to grow opaque with the strength of my headlights, turned its head back to the direction it was walking and finished slowly sauntering across the asphalt. It was as if it was pleased we had in some way recognized its presence and that our fear stroked its ego; it didn't need to do anything else. My sister and I weren't quite sure what to do or what we had just seen. I desperately wanted to slam on the acceleration and get the hell out of there, but at the same time I didn't want to drive through the path of something I felt had some strange evil authority over me... I didn't want it to jump back out at my car.

My sister quickly slapped my hand that was melted over the stick shift, "What are you waiting for!" She clenched her hand down upon mine and yelped, "Get the heck out of here before that thing looks in through the shadows at the side of the car!" Though we no longer saw the entity, we knew it still existed and now we wondered where it was. It had seen us, recognized us, maybe it would come back. I pressed my foot to the floor and screeched past the house that had earlier slowed me down on our adventure toward the small cemetery on the hill. After the adrenaline had passed and the butterflies in our stomachs had pushed up the knot in our throats, we almost started laughing at the sure sign we were bound to experience something tonight. The spirits were active!

"What in the hell was that thing? Have you ever seen anything like it! That's what a shadow man is, that was a shadow person!" My sister was talking in quick gulps as she disproved all those flimsy Hollywood tales and poor excuses for a shadow person and what was likely to be faulty camerawork. She raised her finger to the top of the car and shouted, "That was it! That's what we wanted!" Indeed, we had wanted to have some type of experience so that our money spent at the gas station and our time away from home was not in vain. We hadn't even reached our haunted destination and had already had one of the strangest experiences we shared together to date. I now had seen two shadow people in my lifetime.

We shared the encounter back-to-back like a small game of table ping-pong. She would explain how she had grabbed my thigh and I would jump in with my reaction. We both swapped theories on what shadow men were and had nearly forgotten where we were, nearly passing the turnoff altogether for the cemetery at the top of the hill.

I screeched my brakes for the second time that night and performed a small U-turn over the gravel road. As the small rocks cracked under my tires, my sister asked to stop the car. She had to pee. We were going from a residential neighborhood that was predominantly well-lit to a very dark stretch of road. Every quarter mile or more had a very strong streetlight that gave a sense of security, but we were about to leave that all behind. The street we were about to turn on didn't have any streetlights at all. Ominous lights from the adjacent highway beamed down to illuminate the awning of trees that we would be driving through. We could see the turnoff only because it was the only place the trees parted for a small moment, and also the only place the asphalt crackled into an old gravel road.

As my sister jumped out of the car, I turned off the ignition just a moment to center myself. Cars were whisking by overhead just a few hundred feet away and I could feel the wind rushing over me. It was a beautiful late June evening in Missouri, and to our surprise there was little humidity.

We couldn't see the stars because of the light pollution given off by the local businesses, but we could tell we were on the cusp of the city into suburbia. I often like to close my eyes and think of the history in that exact location. Maybe this exact place in the gravel was home to buffalo or maybe it intermingled with local paths of Lewis and Clark as they shared their own adventure down this way. Just as I was deep in trance, my sister quickly pounded on the roof of the car.

"Oh my God, Sarah! Do you hear that?" She was buttoning up her pants as she danced around the car and hunched over near me. "Listen, listen … What do you hear?"

For a moment, I didn't hear anything. I wanted to remind my sister that she was in a vulnerable position having just peed on the side of the road and perhaps was being spooked by something else. My subconscious desperately dug for a joke I knew was there, but before I could laugh it off my sister once again scolded me over her shoulder and interjected, "No no seriously, listen! You don't hear that?"

I was almost condescending at this point and tried to assure my sister that I didn't hear anything at all, but before I could speak ... I did hear something. A slow drumming seemed to be in the background. I tried to rationalize just what I was hearing and thought maybe the highway noises were creating pareidolia in my mind and I was just thinking I was hearing drumming. I knew I had not validated my sister's experience at this point so I asked her first, "What do you hear?"

My sister threw me a condescending glance. "You know you hear the drumming. You can't not hear that!" Just as I lowered my ego long enough to validate that my sister was not crazy, it occurred to me that this was something I had read previously that night during my Internet research of this area. Many residential people had complained of local drumming for which they could not find a source. For those too skeptical to believe it could be the drumming of an earlier civilization lingering in the land, they blamed the nearby comedy club. Nonetheless, here I was hearing very loud drumming I could no longer refute.

We turned on our handheld recorders to see if the audio would show up later upon analysis. Maybe we were still riding our adrenaline wave out from our earlier experience. However, we both agreed, despite no rational or logical explanation, we were hearing drumming. We both got into the car and smiled at each other. The drumming had a soothing happiness to it. It was a connection to an earlier time and to a history that my sister and I both felt a strong sense of family with. We were pleased to have such a positive paranormal encounter before turning in to the dark woods that would lead us to the cemetery at the top of the hill.

My tires continued to crackle as we drove into the line of trees and into the darkness. The moonlight and occasional overhead plane would light the trees above us, but the only light we were depending on was the high beams of my car on the small gravel path. As we rolled forward at a slow pace, the branches seemed to pull us in as we crept forward mile after mile. We weren't really sure where we were going. The only reason we knew we were approaching the right place was because we could see the airport lights and terminal head-quarters getting closer in the distance. We drove until we could drive no further and had to make the decision to go left or right. One road seemed to disappear down the hill, and we could see some houses off in the distance. If we turned left, however, the road seemed to creep around the edges of the airport property and didn't really look to go anywhere in particular. We turned left.

Frozen in Time

There was a dark haze in the air as if fog were settling or mixing with the gravel dust, and it all glowed a strange hue of orange as the light danced through the clouds from the red airport signals nearby. Using my headlights almost made the visibility of the road more dangerous and difficult to drive, so we turned off all of our lights and focused on the line in the road, made from where the gravel met grass. Eventually we came upon a small cemetery on the top of the hill just as described in all of those forums, the old tales, and the rumors we had heard over the years. Many people claimed to see orbs, dancing lights, or even real-time streams (actual visual anomalies that look like streaming lights) in and around the cemetery property; we only saw lights from the airport in the distance and quickly felt a bit disappointed that maybe this whole journey had been for naught. As we slowly crept upon the small path that led to the cemetery, I asked my sister if she wanted to walk or drive onto the premises. There was no private property signage posted or any warnings against trespassing, and either one seemed to be appropriate since we weren't familiar with our surroundings. We decided we would drive as far as we could and then get out and walk.

As we approached the edge of the cemetery where the tombstones became very visible over the front of my car, we decided to put the vehicle into park and gather our items. We noticed right away that the idle of my car started to sound "off." My headlights and dashboard lights flickered as if a fuse were going out. Before I let the experience get the better of my nerves I turned off my car and pulled the emergency brake.

We reached behind the seats and made sure our flashlights had fresh batteries, and then recorded our introduction onto our digital recording device.

"This is Sarah, the year is 2008, and we are at the cemetery at the top of the hill found at the edge of the airport property. There is no sign letting us know the family plot or direct address of this location…" I described as much as I could about the location since we weren't sure what to call it. My sister and I casually caught eyes and grinned at each other as we pulled on the door handle to get out to investigate. The doors were locked. That was funny; I hadn't locked the doors. We laughed at the blunder and I reached for the unlock button; "flunk," the button released my door.

"Just kidding, let's give this another try!" My sister and I both lunged forward and again found the doors were locked. This time I was a little concerned, because my vehicle was mostly an electric model and almost everything in the vehicle was controlled by an electric button or a computer chip. There were no handles, levers, or manual ways to do much of anything, to my dismay. "Okay, this is a first," I murmured under my breath to my sister.

"Do you think this is a sign?" My sister was always the more superstitious of us. I glared at her over my shoulder and convinced her I was more concerned about a Stephen King novel coming to life than I was worried about some spirit taking over my Ford. Again we tried to laugh off the situation and I jiggled my car door until it opened. As my door released so did my sister's, and though we had been so vigorously awaiting our escape from the small car, neither one of us seemed to want to put our foot to the gravel. Intuitively, we both just sat in the car with the doors wide agape.

"Why don't you go ahead and check things out while I stay here in my newly possessed car," I exclaimed. I thought for sure my sister would agree; she was always more of an introvert and loner and definitely the braver of the two of us. I'm not sure if it is the Leo in her that gives her the blind courage, or perhaps the quality I have always envied, her deep spiritual faith. Instead of my prediction that she would take the bait and investigate by herself, she turned around. "Sarah,

I don't think were supposed to be here. I think there may have been something to all those ghost stories and a real reason that people believe this place is haunted. It doesn't look like much, but I instinctively do not want to get out of this car."

The psychologist in me always loved moments like this. Was I going to try to talk her out of something her intuition was telling her not to do, or should I be the honorable and noble paranormal investigative partner that encourages her to do nothing that makes her uncomfortable? Some part of me always wants that person I am with to get grabbed off into the shadows by something so that I can be a true believer of something spiritually profound. Despite all my experiences up to this point, each and every experience is always new and I'm always waiting for that life-changing piece of evidence that could alter any skeptic's point of view. I didn't, however, want something to grab my sister, and I definitely didn't want to be left all alone with my car acting up.

I drew a deep sigh. "Well if something is telling you that there is danger then we should listen. It could be that we get arrested by airport security, who knows!" I didn't want to instigate my sister any further, and even though I did want to get out of the car, I guess I was a little scared too.

We stayed in the safety of the car and closed the doors behind us. We collected all of our paranormal tools and gadgets and threw them into the backseat. I pressed my foot onto the brake to turn the keys into the ignition. Nothing.

It was at that moment that the pit of my stomach became bottomless. Maybe my sister was right, maybe the tall, dark slender man, the drumming, and my vehicle locking us inside were indeed all signs after all; we were not supposed to be here. Without completely becoming frantic, I simply took the keys out of the ignition and my feet off of the brake and smiled at my sister as I did the whole routine again. Just as I do every day numerous times, I put my foot on the brake, inserted the keys, and cranked the ignition. Nothing. The keys turned in the ignition and all I heard was a click, still nothing.

My sister buried her face in her hands and I could tell she was frustrated and scared but could do nothing just sitting in the passenger seat. Now, being the daughter of a mechanic means that I am always open to the idea of jumping under the hood of my car if I feel like there's an issue at hand. This time, I can tell you that was the last thing I wanted to do!

As I continued to turn my keys, praying this was all some intergalactic joke, the tombstones in the cemetery began to change in a way that is difficult to describe. It was as if heat was coming up from the ground and the images of the headstones were moving. It was like watching an illusion of hope dance across a desert road but instead these were old headstones flickering in place, and this was not "hope." It was a cool summer night and I didn't dare rationalize the experience. I simply wanted to get out of there right now!

My sister and I were almost baffled to the point of sitting frozen in our seats. I must've been unconsciously turning the ignition over, because out of nowhere the wheels began to spin in place and the engine roared. My foot was still on the brake, the emergency brake was still firmly in place but yet my car had started up and the engine was accelerating. I pumped the brake, grabbed the steering wheel, and released the emergency brake. The car accelerated into the cemetery and immediately turned, just barely missing a headstone. We peeled out in the gravel and tore away down the road back the way we had come.

A billowing bowl of frisky gravel rambled behind us as I drove faster than I care to admit. I wasn't worried about going into the ditch, crashing my car into one of the trees, or hitting a large hole where the road was missing, but instead wanted to get as far away from the cemetery as possible. It was all I could think about.

What could have the power to kill my car and lock us inside? I suddenly could empathize with my sister's statement that something instinctually wanted us to leave that cemetery.

Normally, after a paranormal investigation or any paranormal experience my sister and I laugh it off and come back to a positive and grounded place. We take notes about the experience before chatting about it and only after we have put our pens down do we share the experience with each other. This was a habit we had done over the years to protect the viability of our evidence; it was not only as good practice if we were investigating as a team, but it also validated any intuitive or psychic experience we may have had.

Once I came to the end of the gravel road and reached the edge of the tree line again, near the humming highway and buzz of civilization, I stopped the car. We both frantically scribbled notes our papers and I could hear my sister's breath as we rushed through documenting what had just happened. After a few moments of scratching down our notes we looked up, and without a usual smile, swapped notes and began reading. I could read her chicken scratch and was amazed to see how she had described the freaky experience.

Both my sister and I had seen the same thing. We had described similar images, emotions, and both felt an overwhelming sensation of fear and distrust. We had both psychically described the feeling of a male entity being present and taking possession over the property. There may not have been a "no trespassing" sign posted there, but clearly someone was standing by to make sure no one entered the cemetery grounds. I found it interesting that though we did not experience the lights so many before us had, we did experience a strange visual hallucination of some type, because my sister described the headstones as glitching and I seemed to see them in the daze of an energy transfer; like a hazy mirage was appearing over the headstones.

When all was said and done, there was no logical explanation or rational conclusion that we could come to. We simply decided to nod in agreement to those who might say this location is haunted. We can't say by what, or by who, or give much definitive evidence... but we can empathize with a very terrifying experience that to this day we are not sure how to explain.

One fun fact about this unique outing was that our audio evidence did record the drumming off in the distance, and it also recorded some strange howling outside the cemetery that we had not heard when we were present. I've long since considered heading back up to the cemetery on the hill to see if anything would greet me as it had that dark night with my sister.

FOURTEEN

Past Life Experience

I find that there is both a peace and also a great fearful disturbance when that which we thought was a spiritual mystery becomes real. Because this book is compiled of short stories of some of my own haunted experiences, I have to also include that they're not terribly frightening or full of morbid detail, but the reason that they are scary, especially to me, is because they are real. Sometimes the scariest things in our nightmares don't appear as some blood-gurgling clown, but instead it might be seeing the loss of a loved one or the image of loss.

By the time I was in my mid-teens, I had already seen at least three people die right in front of me and had been to more than ten funerals; some of which were for family who were very dear to me. I had been to the funerals of my parents' drug addict friends, acquaintances of the church, grandparents, and even peers that were my age. My father saw to it that

I was brought up in a devoutly Christian home, yet, from my mother, I also had a strong sense of spirituality.

I was raised to believe there was something to the other side and to our afterlife, but there was never really any faith. I was terrified that the eternity described in the Bible both did and did not exist. I had not spoken with God, I had not seen angels, but I had seen people die, and I had felt the presence and seen the images of some scary ghosts. I just wasn't sure there was a divine justification in it all, and it wasn't until I had a past life regression that my spirituality made an incredible change for the better, and with that change, the paranormal got that much darker.

The Hypnotist

My sister and I typically worked the psychic fair twice a year in Kansas City doing psychic readings and leading workshops on the paranormal. Hundreds and even thousands of people traveled all across the country to attend this particular fair due in part because of the vast collection of metaphysical vendors and consumers that would be present. Some world-renowned psychics occasionally showed up and there would be antiques from Egypt to India in some of the small corner booths; it was a metaphysical treasure.

My sister and I mostly loved to work the psychic fair because it was a family tradition, and also because it seemed to help us validate others' abilities and validate ourselves. It was mostly entertaining for me and I loved to network with people that didn't ostracize me for my strange happenings and beliefs.

Some of the vendors were there every year, year after year, and became kind of a sideshow family for my sister and me.

One of the vendors was an old man, hairy from head to toe, and always reminded me of a J.R.R. Tolkien character living in the modern world. He had a long beard that he would sometimes braid, and his tan and callused skin was a stark contrast to his mystically cloudy blue eyes. He worked at the rock booth and his passion in life was to travel the world, collect some of its stones and minerals, polish them up, and find them homes with psychic people all over the globe. He always had a fun story to tell and great treasures on his table.

I remember gazing over a few stones in particular that had caught my eye. He, of course, interrupted to tell me the story of how he had swam with sharks on that particular trip when he had found the stones; he gave them a personality and a special story. He had mentioned perhaps I was drawn to them because I was associated with them in some past life and therefore "must" be reconnected.

That phrase, "a past life," was always thrown around with my mother and all of her metaphysical friends. Sure, I knew about the Indian belief system of reincarnation and I also knew that the human body was biodegradable. At the basic belief of it all, how could I deny that some part of us goes on after death?

It was very difficult for me to not laugh when hearing others describe their special past life connections. The life they had with some famous person; someone they believed they had lived with so many hundreds of years earlier. I really wanted to go to Paris, I was definitely attracted to Hindu gods,

I also loved deep Southern Cajun food and voodoo dolls, but I wasn't about to declare those parts about myself as being related to a past life. When the old man saw that I rolled my eyes at his comment he got more serious than I had ever seen him. He looked at me for a moment and after a long and awkward silence called out, "You mean to tell me you don't believe in past lives?" He scorned me and seriously changed from his happy, frumpy self to a seriously concerned mentor of a man.

It was as if he had heard my entire inner monologue and rant against the whole silly idea. Perhaps he was just intuitive enough or had known me long enough to gather what I thought was bullshit. He leaned over the table of stones and lightly slapped my upper shoulder, "Hell, I guess I get it. But before you write the whole thing off, you need to go see Jean!" He pointed to a woman just two tables down from his own vendor area.

I had seen the booth before and I also recognized the older woman with the chic white bob; she was also a regular at these fairs. Unlike most people that seem to catch eyes from one conference to another, she did not ever introduce herself, and we never shared even a small conversation.

"Yeah maybe I will," I said with a chuckle.

"No I'm serious girl," he clambered about, "she is the real deal Holyfield."

I laughed at his analogy and bought the stone I had been fingering in my hands during the whole discussion. He wrapped my stones in his unique paper and passed it under the skull in the back of his booth. The skull was an acquired "conversation piece" that the old man attested was a relic. It had divine powers and alien origins and would "charge" the stones after the purchase. You couldn't help but stare at it from across the booth. Dark, hollow eyes that followed you from one end of the room to the other. It *did* seem supernatural, and who was I to deny this old man's tale of its power? He passed the "charged" items to me and gave me far more change than I needed back, then he winked at me. "Do it."

On the last day of the fair my sister asked me what I hadn't purchased yet. During our breaks from doing readings, we would circle the fair and usually pick out items we added to a "wish list." On the first day we would take note of any and every item we wanted, and a few items we thought we "needed." On the second day, we would do the route again and see what items had been saved by divine intervention and not purchased from the floods of people the day before. On the third day, we not only knew the item was meant to be if it had remained unpurchased through the crowds of consumers but also that was the last day of the fair, and the item would shortly be on sale. I couldn't help but notice the sign for past life readings on Jean's booth.

"I've been thinking about maybe ... well, I might get one of these readings over here; what do you think?" I bumped shoulders with my sister and pointed in the direction of the past life readings and the colorful sign. My sister had been interested in the soul songs the musician was offering at the booth adjacent to Jean's, so we almost unconsciously sauntered in that direction.

"Oh, do it! I'll get one, too, and we can go together!" My sister had a positive skip in her step and was excited to hand over money for a past life reading. That in itself is a very unique experience, because my sister is typically never jolly and never enjoys giving out money; but who does? The purchase of our reading was quite casual and didn't include any explanation at all. Jean simply handed me her business card and let me know to call her within the next few days to set up our appointment. We had explained we would like to do the readings together and she agreed that was just fine.

I actually didn't call her to make that appointment until a few weeks after the fair. I was intrigued, but a little disappointed I had spent money; I think possibly I was also a little scared to give her a call. I knew the past life readings that Jean offered were done through hypnosis and were not like a general psychic reading, and I had never been hypnotized before.

Some psychics will simply tell you about your past life. You sit down, they read your energy, and then you listen as they spin a beautiful and wonderful tale. You may or may not find any linking coincidences or even points of interest, but typically the stories are so beautiful you're proud to call them a part of your own. This past life reading wasn't like that; Jean insisted she wouldn't say a thing and that the experience would come completely from my own subconscious.

I picked my sister up and we stopped by a local drive-in to get a slushy for the long drive to Jean's. We would be driving almost an hour and a half to visit Jean at her home just outside of Kansas. We drove over the state line, danced to '80s music on the radio, and were both very anxious and excited for our first past life experience. My sister had brought her handheld recorder so that she could record both of the readings for us.

My sister was always thinking about things like that. In the days before GPS or cellular phones that gave turn-by-turn directions, directions were often screeched out to the driver from chicken scratch written on the back of a paper plate. At least that's what my sister and I used to do when we would ask Dad for directions. The directions weren't always accurate, and occasionally we found ourselves lost and asking a gas station attendant where exactly we were, as was such the case in this experience.

My sister and I were nervous that by arriving fifteen minutes late to Jean's home she may not honor our appointment. Instead she happily greeted us at the door and appeared much softer than she had in the environment of the psychic fair. She was wearing a soft blue robe adorned with turquoise jewelry and her stark white bob cut was more wispy and relaxed. Her house was decorated with Native American murals that illustrated wolves and eagles all through the home. Dreamcatchers, moccasins, arrowheads, and other culturally spirited items adorned the tabletops and hallways as we walked from the front door to the living space. The home was quite large and very expensive.

Down the Rabbit Hole

Jean directed us to the fluffy leather couch and offered us a drink. My sister and I both happily obliged to her iced tea.

We all joined together in the living room to talk about the past life regression that was going to take place. Jean quite bluntly asked us what our religion was as she slipped off her shoes and sat cross-legged in her chair across from us. At this time in my life, I was very unfamiliar with neurolinguistic programming and any hypnosis-speak. She spoke of imprints, values, and why people typically repress their past lives. She described how past lives have been discovered through hypnotherapy and introduced us to some authors to research further after our session.

Looking back on the experience now, I'm quite impressed with her professionalism, as she was clear to mention the risk involved with having a past life regression. She illustrated that the experience could shake you to your very foundation and leave you questioning your faith if you weren't prepared. We explained that though we were raised in a Southern Baptist culture we were also extremely spiritual.

I had agreed to have my past life regression first and so we climbed the staircase to an office upstairs at the end of the hall. I remember taking each step up to that room, because the carpet was so soft that I sank a little with each step. I looked at the portraits of family members that decorated the hallway and remember how peaceful the office was when we stepped in. It smelled slightly of cinnamon and lavender and the light was dim and soft. There was just a little white noise of running water in the back of the room and she had assured us no one would be home to disturb the session.

My sister found a dark corner in the room to get comfortable and turn on her hand recording device. I remember I could always hear her breathing through my session, a sort of anchor to reality. Jean looked me in the eyes, held her hands over mine, and encouraged me to slow down and deepen my breaths. I sat upon on a soft massage chair and stared up at the ceiling while Jean perched next to me in a chair. When she could tell that my body and mind was more relaxed she guided me to lie down on the massage table in the middle of the room. She sat in a chair next to me and her mouth was level to my ears just a few feet away. She spoke softly, calmly, and in a very monotone voice. She guided me through a short protection spell and a visualization of relaxing my body. For the regression, she walked me down a flight of colorful stairs.

In my mind's eye I was asked to walk down a staircase and with each stair I would go deeper into my consciousness and the colors began to change. We started at the top of the staircase where everything was red and grounding. She then moved me through the colors of the rainbow, or chakras, and led me down the staircase. She counted down, she spoke more slowly, and the visualization was very relaxing.

It was at that point Jean asked me to visualize a long hallway with doors stretching as far as I could see. Upon her request, I could imagine a long hallway such as one found in a motel and could see door after door after door. She then asked my subconscious to illuminate a door to a past life that would provide me with a meaningful and positive experience. She asked me if any door lit up or grabbed my attention in particular...and one already had. I remember it was an older wooden door and the knob was a Victorian-decorated bronze handle. I had never seen a door like this in person, but I could describe every little detail.

I reached out to turn the handle and could see my feet stepping over the light that shone from underneath the doorway. I turned the doorknob completely and stepped inside the room. Jean requested that I describe the room I was in, but to her and to my dismay, I could simply see the back of my eyelids; darkness. I didn't see anything at all, just darkness. It was at this moment I really wanted to sit up and request my money back, to tell her it just hadn't worked on me, and agree that hypnosis was a very subjective thing. She asked me again, "Sarah, what do you see?"

I took a deep breath in, I combated with my conscience on whether to let the cat out of the bag that I was not really hypnotized; if someone came running in the room screaming "fire" I could easily get up and run to safety. I knew where I was, I felt the table underneath me, and I could still hear my sister breathing in the corner. Jean asked me again, "Sarah, could you describe the room to me?"

"I don't see anything; it's just darkness," I mumbled under my breath.

"I would like for you to reach for a light source. You need to find a way to light the room. Feel around...create light...and described the room you see." Jean seemed to be quite sure that I was hypnotized and so I figured I would entertain her for the sole fact that I had already paid my money, I had already driven over an hour, and I knew that my sister was excited for the subtle process to really work. Well, so was I. I took a deep breath and tried to find the "right" answer.

"Well, I guess I'll feel around for a light switch then." I wanted to laugh and I half-hoped Jean did not sense my condescending nature. So I imagined myself feeling around in the darkness for a light switch or something that would "light the room." I pretended to feel the light switch under my fingers and, sure enough, flipped the switch upward to the sky. I could imagine a room in my mind and would have no problem describing it.

"I see an older cabin in the woods. There's some older upholstered furniture in the corner and a large window on the wall facing me." I could see the room completely and if she had asked, I could have described everything from the carpet to the peeling of the wallpaper over the walls.

"Very good. Now I'd like you to walk over to the window, take a long look outside, and describe for me what you see." Jean continued to talk softly and guided me with no suggestive tips on how to explore my realm.

"I don't see anything in particular," I exclaimed. "Just some normal trees and the ground looks like it might be covered with mulch, it's not grass, I do know that. The sky is blue like any other day, the windows are somewhat older, because the paned glass is thicker than usual, and I suppose I don't really have any attachment to where I am at." I tried to describe every detail I could think to create in my mind and I was being honest; I didn't really have any emotions at all toward the picture

I was painting in my mind. I'm not sure where it was coming from and I even tried to hesitate and decide if this was a regurgitated movie from my childhood or if I was just being creative. Again, I had thought I should sit up and let everyone know I was making this up! I was just answering questions with whatever came to mind; it wasn't "real." Or was it?

"How about you turn and walk out of this room. Let's explore the rest of the building that you are in. Describe for me exactly what you're seeing and if you happen to recall the year or the city. I would love to know exactly where you are!" Jean sounded so excited and so genuinely concerned about learning the details of my vision. I entertained her.

"Well, as I'm walking out of this room the door looks like any other. I no longer see the doorknob I once turned to get into this place and the beautiful Victorian bronze knob is no longer here. The carpet is not thick or plushy, but it is some type of matted carpet under my feet and there's not really any noise. The house is quiet; I'm the only one home. Perhaps everyone is asleep. I'm still not sure what city we're in, because I don't remember ever seeing any street signs to identify our travels. Interesting, I said 'our' ... I wonder why that is?" I openly began narrating my vision. I still didn't have any emotional attachment to what was popping into my mind, but I decided to not only entertain Jean, but to entertain my own imagination. Perhaps I could concoct some amazing story for a book to be published later in my life. Maybe this was a guided meditation?

"Now I'm walking into a living space, everything is very neat and orderly. I can tell I'm a bit controlling about how everything looks but it's only to control my anxiety. I still don't feel any strong emotional attachment and this definitely is not someplace I would call a home. I do feel as though other people live here with me, but no one seems to be around."

"Wonderful job. Could you tell me your name, or describe who you are? Your gender, your age; what can you tell me about yourself?" Jean asked politely.

Almost instantly I seemed to have the ability to describe this new character that had just popped into my mind with excruciatingly fine detail. I didn't have to think about how it would work for the plot or storyline I was creating, but it just somehow appeared. I was an older woman, perhaps in my early fifties, and I was exhausted. I was spiritually exhausted. I remember exactly how it felt. That's when I realized, as I was describing this person I was in my vision, I did have some kind of emotional attachment.

"I have light brown hair pulled into a messy knot behind me, and I'm well-groomed, and in an outfit I probably have worn a thousand times because it was picked out for me. I couldn't tell you how much I weigh, what my career is, because something is missing, and I feel absolutely worthless. I really despise who I am on a very deep level and being in this body, feeling this way, is a bit overwhelming." I began to speak slower, breathing shallower, even though details were streaming at me. I could answer any question as if I *was* this character and I did feel attached. I kept wondering what movie this was that

I hadn't watched for all these years that had left such a mark on me and my childhood. It was then that Jean asked me to locate other family members. She asked me if I had seen any pictures in the home and if so to walk toward them.

"Yes, there are pictures hung in the living room on the wall. They're all lined perfectly in an organized fashion and are all framed in the same dark wooden frame. There is my son!" I pointed to the pictures on the wall that I could so perfectly see in my mind's eye and described each of the people in them. I knew their names, their careers, their ages, strange quirky behavior mannerisms of each person, and scariest of all I had no idea where this was coming from.

"How wonderful," Jean said. "Are you in any of these photos?"

After a long and depressing pause, I answered. "No."

"Why not? You are the mother? Why are you not in any of these pictures?"

I began to uncontrollably sob. Many would jokingly call it the "ugly cry," because it's the kind of crying where you want to curl up in a fetal position and empty your body of all its fluids; tears streaming down your face so heavily you cannot see. I felt a lump in my throat shaking with each attempt to describe my sadness, and at the same time I was consciously thinking, *What the hell is the matter with you Sarah?* Part of me was very embarrassed. I didn't really cry in front of my sister and I especially didn't cry, not like this, in front of a complete stranger. I was aware that I was crying and I couldn't stop. Jean let me cry for a few moments and then softly spoke, "At the count of three I want you to stop crying. Instead, I would love for you to calmly explain to me why this makes you so sad. One ... Two ... Three."

And as if years had passed, I suddenly didn't feel sadness anymore and I could gain composure. I was desperate to maintain composure just moments before but could not grasp my sanity. Now, at the count of a stranger, I was okay again. But a part of me was in shock. What had just happened? Before I had much time to process and think about this whole experience I was already answering Jean's question. At this point, I realized I was just disassociatively talking, and though I wasn't sure where this was coming from, I was going to let it entertain me too. I sat back deep within my subconscious and listened. I was done trying to consciously explain and organize this information and was just going to let it come out. Perhaps this was some deep catharsis that I needed. I was going to ride the wave and let this happen.

"I'm not in any of these pictures because of the shame that I carry. I had the perfect family and it has all been taken away from me. What was left, I ruined." I said this with a deep sorrow. I could feel an emptiness within me.

"I'm so sorry to hear that," Jean said. "Why don't we talk a little bit about how this came to be? Can you give me a brief story of your life so far? What happened to you? Let me listen," she calmly requested.

"My parents were very rich. I was the only daughter and I was treated as such; spoiled nearly every day of my life. I felt love from many people, in many ways, and yet I never knew exactly what love was until I had met my husband. I was shopping at a local market in town and came upon him as he was selling his fruits and vegetables. He was so handsome I could barely take my eyes off of him. We noticed each other right away and smiled from across the market. It was a connection that I had missed and I knew we were meant for one another. I remember how his hair grew long over his eyes and I would always brush it away so that I could see his beautiful brown eyes.

"He was a very hard worker, helped to take care of his brothers, and was a kind man. We were both a little young but each and every time the market was in town we seemed to share the date fondly. Though we had not known each other long, after a few months we decided to get married. I broke all traditions. My family was to choose my husband and it was to be a political event. People in the wealthy class married for convenience and for family wealth, not for petty things like love. I knew this man that I had fallen so deeply in love with would not be allowed to be in my life if I asked permission so I chose instead to ask for forgiveness.

"My parents had no forgiveness for me. They shunned me, and though I was their only child, they threw me out onto the street to go live with my new husband. They didn't want anything to do with me and were ashamed of my decision."

I continued to describe our marriage, how we struggled to live with one another financially, but how we were completely happy, and how wonderful it felt to have a connection with someone who didn't judge. I felt at home and I was madly in love. Though I was frightened and unprepared, we also had a young son. I described how badly I had wanted to introduce him to my parents, but again, that I had been exiled from the life I once knew. My husband and I struggled to make ends meet, but we always ended each day with a smile. I had my complaints, but I couldn't be happier. Then I noticed as I continued the tale that it got much harder to speak. My heart grew heavy and my breath grew short. I stopped narrating my story. I just felt sorrow.

"Then what happened?" Jean waited a moment and then asked me what changed in that life.

The knot grew once again in my throat and tears streamed down my cheeks. "He died. He left me." I began to sob on the table once more and felt a loss beyond compare. Jean patted me on the shoulder and handed me a Kleenex as I continued to cry.

After a few moments of grieving she finally reached for my hand and said, "Take me to a later time. How did things work out after he passed?"

"After my husband died I couldn't take care of our small child. In this time and age an unmarried woman could simply do nothing. I showed up at the doorstep of my parents as a last resort. When they learned of my husband's death they seemed excited. My father almost immediately married me to an older man within his fraternity group; an old pig of a man! He was nearly twenty years older and his waistband was larger around than he was tall. He always had a small amount of crust built in the corners of his mouth as he never stopped talking politics and rarely took effort to keep himself clean.

"I was disgusted with him both physically and emotionally. Every day away from my husband pretending to be married to another man was the most unloyal and shameful thing I could do. The worst of it was that my family demanded we tell the world that my son was this new man's offspring. I was to play this horrible role in a production that demeaned the whole love I had previously found. I was so disgusted that it took every ounce of energy to get up out of bed each morning and I did this for years. For eternity."

"What happened to your son?" Jean asked. "You loved your son so much, what happened?"

Tears began to stream down my face once more, but I could speak. "I knew a young child could not keep such a secret so everyone simply told him he was Gary's son and he never knew the truth. I would look in his eyes and see the love of my life staring back at me with disappointment. I began drinking. I began drinking so heavily that I just lay in bed all day; the staff raised my family and did my errands. I simply did not care. After the horrible sham of a life that I had lived in the wake of my husband's death ... I just couldn't take it."

"Do you want to experience how you ended this life?" Jean asked.

"I already know. There's no one in the house today, because this is the day I decided to go out to the cabin at the lake to shoot myself. I knew right where Gary kept his gun in the top dresser drawer of the office, and I knew my son wouldn't have to see me. There would be a mess, but no one would see, no one would know, and the staff could make it all better before my son saw. I did shoot myself that day and I was glad to do it."

As I described the end, my suicide, I felt as if I knew this person. I was this person. I empathized on a deeper level than I ever thought possible and I could recollect this story in its entirety; I didn't have to give a short summary. I knew these people, I knew their traditions, and it was amazing. Having told the end of the story I was released from my sofa in the corner of my mind and I could begin to process what had just happened. Was this one of my past lives? This was not a famous person or a positive story, but I knew it was mine.

"Sarah, I would like to meet your soul mates in this life-time. I would like to go through the man that is your hus-band, Gary, and your son, and see who they are today in your present life. Would that be okay?" As Jean asked this question, I was once again on the backseat roller coaster ride of an adventure simply answering in a flash. I illus-trated that I still hadn't touched base with my husband and I wasn't sure who that was in my present life, but I did know Gary. Most importantly, my son ... the little boy I had aban-doned, was currently my present boyfriend Brian.

You see, Brian was a beautiful young man that loved to cheat on me. I knew that he slept around, I knew that he called other women, and I especially knew because I had found video evidence of it. Nonetheless, despite my strong and indepen-dent nature, I always would forgive him. Brian could do no wrong! It was probably the one area of my life I was currently most ashamed of; I knew that everyone in my life that had grown to know me as a strong woman was seeing me in a very pitiful role. Brian was using me and I knew it; so did everybody else. Despite it all, I loved him unconditionally and didn't know why. Until now.

"Do you see the lesson?" Jean asked this question and waited.

Nothing came to mind right away. I tried not to think too much and just worked over the process... just repeating her words in my mind. "Did I know the lesson?" Then, out of nowhere, I realized that Brian had been my son. He was the little boy I had lied to all of those years and he was supposed to be my husband's legacy. I never told him about his amazing father and where he'd really come from. Every day I lied to the most important thing in my life and the shame and disgust grew within me each night I lay down to sleep. Here he was, reincarnated, and I was taking care of him. I was making his meals, doing his laundry, and it didn't matter what he did; I owed it to him to be there. I didn't want to fail him again. It made sense! I could never rationalize why I had such a connection with Brian. I could never understand why I would give advice to other women and even curse and yell at television shows illustrating the exact same scenario I was in, but yet I couldn't take action. He was... He was my son.

"Now that you've learned that lesson and you've made those soul connections, I would like for you to meet back with that entity, with that soul... I want you to visualize your son and the life we just experienced. I'm giving you permission to have a moment with him and to tell him what you need to say."

Jean had created a safe haven conference room, so to speak, in my mind. Just as I would do in the future with

therapy clients, this was an opportunity to openly say something I needed to get off my chest. By the time she finished
phrasing the statement, I had already invited my son back in.
I could see him there at my favorite age, no higher than my
waist. I slumped down, my hands on my bent knees, and met
eyes with him. I could see the love for my husband once again,
and I nearly wanted to reach up and brush hair from over his
eyes. I ran my fingers to my son's hair and down around over
his shoulders. I lightly hugged him and said, "I really need to
tell you something." He just looked at me with a smile.

"Your daddy is not Gary. Your daddy was an amazing man
and we were both very much in love ... I still love him. In order
to take care of you, I had to do things I was not happy with
and that meant a lot of lying to you and for that I am so sorry.
I am so sorry. I'm sorry for drinking, I'm sorry for neglecting,
and I'm sorry for not telling you the truth. I'm sorry for being
so selfish I took my own life, and I couldn't be the mom you
deserved."

By the time I had completed my apology I was once again
covered in my own tears. A grand connection had been made
in my soul. Here I was, wondering just how this door, this life,
this past life regression was anything positive and meaningful
as Jean had requested it be. It was sad and it was heartbreak-
ing. But as I apologized to my son and let the forgiveness
wash over me I felt a calloused layer of negativity peel back
from within me.

You see, in my present life my mother was an alcoholic.
After she divorced my dad, she withered into a woman that I

hated. I couldn't understand why she preferred to drink, why she preferred to lie, and why she neglected me and my sister. I just saw her as a very selfish woman and I never felt a connection. Now, having experienced this past life regression, I knew what it felt like to be that mother. I felt a connection.

Not only had my connection with my mother changed in that very instant but also the perception of my current relationship. I had been praying for a way to break it off with Brian and not yearn to be with him or take care of him, and now it all made sense. I could rationalize the reasons why I felt instinctually I needed to take care of him and could also say, "Sarah that was another life and you have to make the better of this one." I could move on and move forward. I no longer questioned myself for my motives or the behaviors I couldn't understand within me and knew there was some divine intervention and reason to it all. I felt peace. I felt excited.

"Now that you've had a moment to accept the peace and forgiveness in your life and learn this life lesson, I would like to venture down the hallway as we had done before and for you to turn another doorknob. Can you see yourself in the hallway of doors now?" Jean once again had teleported my consciousness back to that hallway and that strange motel. I did see the doors and she didn't have to ask for one to light up, the process was already happening.

"Where are you now?"

Interestingly enough, I was relaxed, so I could speak without any hesitation. I didn't question the light or question what was coming to me like I had done before and instead my world was already illuminated. The sun was high in the sky and I was standing in the desert.

Odd as it might seem, as I described myself, I was describing a middle-aged man. A warrior dressed in an amazing warrior outfit. I could describe in complete detail the way my armor looked, the weapons I carried, how my hair was worn, and I could look down and see my sun-kissed hands built with arthritis in every joint. I knew the year, I knew my profession, and even the vocabulary I was using illustrated that I was a warrior of great status and experience. I did describe my family and uniquely I did not have a connection romantically with my wife in that life. We liked each other, we procreated, and I had a son. Again, I had this connection with the son, who I had hoped would not follow in my footsteps and be a warrior. Despite tradition, and despite my culture, I didn't want any harm to come to him. Everything in my life was routine, was strong and metallic, but the love I had for my son was beyond compare.

During the milestones of this life I have described, I illustrated that my son defied my orders and went off to lead an army fighting our enemy. He was a great archer and stepped out in front of the line to get a better sight of his target. He died in the line of duty as a hero for our nation, but at that moment my heart died with him. After the loss of my son, life was much less meaningful. I actually boarded the ship I knew had harbored a traitor and out on the rough ocean water watched my ship be set aflame.

I lay in the under decks of the ship within my captain's quarters on a bed lined with the hide of an animal's fur. I watched the fire break through the ceiling as beams fell all around me, and I could hear the screams of my crew and fellow men. I watched the water, and felt it move over my body as the ship sank and I drowned. I wanted more to meet my son in the afterlife than I did to avenge anything in my life. And just as before, Jean led me through the process of seeing who those people were in that life and who they currently were in my present life. I described this lifetime in amazing detail and after nearly an hour, we explored the life lessons once again.

"I know who my son was; it is my dad now. I know his soft and kind energy and his ability to want to do good for others over all else. He wants to please everyone, but he is defiant and must do it his own way." I softly spoke in a very prideful voice about my father and just as before, all the connections began to make sense. I knew why I always felt such a strong connection with my dad despite him often being away at work. I never quite felt as if I was "under" my father (hierarchly speaking) such as a child is to a parent, but instead felt a comradery. Jean allowed me to explore my life lesson and also to speak to anyone I needed to talk to. I got to say my piece, reflect on my actions, and again, another calloused layer of my soul peeled away and I felt liberated. I felt more alive and aware.

Where It All Comes From

I've written stories since I was a child. I've told tales, exaggerated nightmares, and yet never before have I gotten such peace from a story that had come from my mind. I wasn't definitively sure if this was a past life, because I wasn't sure exactly what that meant. I can tell you without question that the connections I had in the stories I told lived within my mind as my own memories; they were a part of my soul. I felt them, I knew them, and they made sense to me.

Spiritually speaking, it was an amazing experience. I now could understand just what that hairy old man at the stone vendor table was talking about. As if I wasn't already confused before my past life regression, now I wasn't sure how to put this all into my religion or my faith, because the Bible didn't talk about anything like this. My experience in past lives was unlike anything that was depicted in a Hindu or even an Egyptian culture of reincarnation. I didn't feel like there is any karmic punishment or reward, but just that you learn and grow. I asked Jean what she thought of the whole experience and what she had learned through leading people through their past lives.

"For the same reason we go to school starting at kindergarten and then graduate someday many years down the road, we have the summers off and we also meet with our teacher to discuss what will be learning that school year. If we work hard, we put in the work, we put in the time, and we move on and move up from grade to grade. We also find we gravitate toward some of our schoolmates and those peers become a friend through the process. I think that's what the Bible is talking about and that God is a teacher. We discuss with the 'teacher' what our lesson will be and perhaps request certain friends help us along the way and eventually we graduate. And just like the Bible says, eventually we stand alongside God in a peaceful heaven and understand the universe with no judgment, because we have lived it in every role possible. It is then we can either relax and transcend (living in His great kingdom He has made for us) or use our enlightenment to go back to school and help others with their process. At least that's what I like to believe," she laughed.

There were lots of gaps, let's be honest, but that story was nice and it appeased my questions for the time being. I have used this very same analogy with many of my past life clients as now I am the hypnotherapist. The reason this experience is here with these paranormal stories is because so much of the paranormal is about our spirit and the spirit of others. It's also about faith and learning and understanding that not everything is as empirical as we like it to be. It's also about the belief in something that doesn't conform and might just be greater than our understanding. It's mysterious, it's beautiful, and now thanks to my past life regression, I also have the faith to know something very real is going on after we die. I don't have faith anymore, I have belief. It has come full circle for me as a therapist, because now, fifteen years later, I lead people down their own past life regressions and I learn from their experiences. I don't always have the answers for people, but I have learned that somewhere, deep within ourselves … we have the answers.

The Lion People

I suppose you're wondering what happened to my sister during her past life regression. Well, that is mostly her story to tell, but what I can tell you is that her experience with past lives opened a door far beyond anything we could have expected. You see, we had our brief run-ins with alien encounters (dreams, lights in the skies, and stories) and the Mutual UFO Network (M.U.F.O.N.) meetings, but nothing was intimately clear to us about a fourth encounter in our lives.

I had reoccurring dreams up to this point, but I had not yet met the doctor (discussed in the next chapter) who would transcend my studies into more ufology scenarios; that would come in five years' time. I was still a teenager, my sister still a young woman, and we knew there was something "out there," but we weren't sure where to begin on how we were connected to such things. My sister's past life was that beginning.

Whereas my past life regression included ordinary lives and ordinary scenarios (though vastly life-changing to me), my sister started off her journey with a big disconnect. I assumed she was experiencing the same doubt and anxiety that I had experienced during my first moments "under" but instead, she was distant. She was distant in a way that she didn't answer Jean's questions and she couldn't come up with answers (creatively imagined or otherwise). She instead seemed to choke over her words and gargle strange sentences aloud. I saw Jean shift in her chair and take a deep breath as she changed her questions to my sister.

"I want you to try to speak to me clearly. Where are you?" she asked my sister.

"I'm somewhere cold. Metallic," my sister slowly murmured. "It's cold and I'm alone. It's not working anymore and I'm stranded."

Just then, my sister started speaking in a strange voice and in a language I had never heard. She wasn't crying and didn't show any emotion at all, though her tonality had changed drastically. It was as if she was channeling something and was no longer my sister here in the room. Both Jean and I began to feel uncomfortable.

"I want you to translate your speech to English. Speak English." Jean requested of my sister.

My sister then went on to tell a strange tale of coming from "another place" and being stranded in a year far from now. Centuries ago she had remembered being left all alone and was describing the vessel she arrived in that no longer worked. After her session was over, Jean had a short conversation with my sister about how she felt during her regression. My sister explained that she was a little envious she didn't have the emotional catharsis she had just watched me have hours earlier and instead of feeling liberated, she felt confused.

Jean suggested she research the Lion People. The Lion People research would be a long jump into the "rabbit hole," as I call it, and it was linked to the belief aliens are among us. Hybrids made from ancient aliens that could be traced to early hieroglyphics; the Lion People were isolated loners among us.

Needless to say, after doing some research, my sister found her identity in this world and has since become an Egyptian theologian who helps others with their spiritual journey; how otherworldly those journeys might be.

FIFTEEN

The UFO Story

I would like to believe that crawling beneath the veil and learning as much from the paranormal as possible means that it's not just about ghosts and hauntings, but it is also about researching what lives beyond in the great outer space. That which is not normal and extends far beyond our reach is the uncanny connection that UFOs seem to have with the paranormal. You can discuss reptilians and Nephilim in the Bible, theories of the Egyptian connection to the Annunaki, or even to speak on present-day experiences with UFO sightings in correlation to the Mothman or omen-type images in society.

UFOs seem to visit in their own way, in their own time, and still remain beyond our grasp of understanding. With millions of encounters a year, aliens and their visits are a very popular theme and theory behind what a haunting or apparition may be. In my experience, there is a very definitive difference.

That may not be something I can illustrate through Mel meter readings or electromagnetic shifts, but the truth is, I believe I have encountered both aliens and ghosts, and in my intuition of their energy I believe their purpose is different.

As you have read, ghosts seem to want to communicate and sometimes even have a sense of humor. There is a human connection to the spirit outside the physical that lead you to them with a certain amount of empathy. Beyond the bumps in the night, shadow people seem to be scary because they have some malicious intent; however, I believe to have intent you also have to have concern. It's the old therapist cliché that to be angry at someone you must first have love for them. I don't believe that ghosts, demons, or even tall, dark, slender figures in the night maliciously would hurt me if I wasn't so important or in some way connected. The alien experience, however, is quite different.

I was in my early twenties when I started actually doing research of my own and following in the footsteps of paranormal researcher and author Hans Holzer. I was desperately trying to wrap my mind around math and physics and had become terribly interested in quantum theory. I was really trying to make all the evidence, found online or by petty paranormal investigators, fit into the scientific method somehow to prove the paranormal. I think at that point in my career I felt a lot of drama, I needed a lot of validation, I was thirsty for knowledge, and I also was always preoccupied with the idea that I needed to prove something, as if to shake all those people who had made fun of me all those years.

It was at that time in my life I was becoming a licensed hypnotherapist and had met a very gifted professor at my university. He and his wife both taught in the psychology department and were founders of the hypnosis group at the university. After taking a handful of classes, they both had learned of my interest in the paranormal and my application of forensic psychology to parapsychology research and had invited me over for dinner. We ate delicious appetizers under the moonlight and talked all night about hypnosis, past life regressions, and UFO stories.

I had retold the tale of my reoccurring dream, and even of the few occurrences I thought maybe I had by chance caught a UFO. We talked about the chupacabra, Bigfoot, and what the heck I might end up doing with my life, having such a strange passion.

The next day in class, my professor handed me a note card. The yellow square of paper had the chicken scratch of a contact, a person I was to interview for my final paper. It read:

"After reading your last paper I know that as a teacher I am more than just red pen markings on paper. I met a guy in college who was one of my colleagues and who shares many of your same passions. He's a great author now on UFOs and alien encounters. You should give him a call and tell him I said hello. In fact, make it an interview for your final paper in this class so that I know you'll do it and do it well."

I laughed at his obligation to make the call an assignment. He knew that in some cases when an authority was so great on a subject I oftentimes felt as though I wasn't on the same level; I would be anxious and hesitate to talk openly about my goals. However, with my stubborn perfectionism on the line, I vowed to call the author and doctor of psychology on the phone to scratch out a time we could talk. To my surprise, the number was actually his cell phone and he answered after his early morning swim.

"Hello? Hello can you hear me?" I could hear him scrambling the phone in his hand as he answered.

"Yes, doctor. Are you there? My name is Sarah, and I'm calling to talk to you about booking a time to have an interview."

"Are you from the paper?" He seemed to think I was a journalist calling to write an article about one of his recent discoveries. He wasn't disappointed when I explained I was just an undergraduate student looking to make a connection with someone in the paranormal field. I was looking to interview him based on the recommendation of my professor at the university and was hoping he had some advice for me. He eagerly announced I would call him the next morning promptly at 7:00 a.m. and that we would spend an hour talking about such things. Before I could let him know that 7:00 a.m. was much too early for me, a young student who was working a full-time job at night while juggling school during the day, he had already hung up the phone.

The next morning I sipped my hot coffee and forced my eyelids open as I sat down at the computer and unplugged my charged phone. I called the doctor again on his cell phone and after nearly seven rings I began to wonder if he meant seven o'clock at night, and here I was waking him up in the morning! Just as I pulled the phone away from my ear to hang up I heard him answer, "Hello? Hello is anyone there?"

"Yes, I'm here doctor. This is Sarah; I called you yesterday."

"Yes, I know who you are, let's get on with it." And without hesitation he asked me what it was I was studying and why we were connected; why had my professor thought he could be of some help. I began to explain that I had grown up in a very haunted house and had a very spiritual mother and sister and religious father that helped mold me into the woman I was. I included my paranormal encounters, my reoccurring alien dreams, and also my time spent with the professional paranormal investigative team out of Kansas City. I illustrated that I had started working for the mental health center and was majoring in psychology but had a deep interest in hypnotherapy and how for some individuals, a paranormal experience was said to be a mental illness; others described it as a spiritual encounter. I wanted to know how I could make this fuzzy passion of mine something more definitive, something that could pay the bills, and most importantly something that could be a legacy of some kind. I described my passion for Hans Holzer, the scientific community, and even my lectures on strange topics such as spontaneous human combustion or cryptozoology. After about thirty minutes of me talking, he finally said something.

"I see," he said under his breath. After that, there was a long and very awkward silence on the phone. "Yes, I see."

"So what can you tell me about the work that you do doctor?" I asked.

"Well, you may or may not have heard of me. I don't subscribe to all the Hollywood flimflam you see on TV these days and I prefer to spend my time doing serious research on the matter. I've written a number of books and my most recent is on alien encounters and the soul samples they take with them; quite frankly the psychology behind why they're taking us. I don't have time to debate whether the topics of my research are valid or not, but instead prefer to work with individuals who support my goal in uncovering the mystery behind abduction. You said you're a psychic?"

I could hardly believe after my thirty minutes of talking and my very brief mention (come to think of it had I even mentioned this?) of being psychic within my discussion of the paranormal that he was asking such a question. "Yes, I would consider myself a sensitive ... "

"Ah, I see."

I laughed with a sort of subtle smile. "Do you feel as though psychic connections somehow play a role with an alien abduction?" I asked.

Again there was a long pause on the phone and I could tell the doctor was really thinking about his answer. "Well, when were you abducted?"

I found it interesting that he didn't ask me if I *had been* but instead asked me *when*; he was so absolutely certain that he had made a statement to ask. "I don't know about all that," I laughed.

"You do understand that you're laughing out of context because that is your defense mechanism. As a psychology student I'm sure you understand the importance of repressing such a memory. They are quite traumatic. I didn't quite think that I had one myself until after years of hypnotherapy, it finally came to fruition. I was so scared of the experience, and so worried that somebody would implant a false memory, I became a licensed hypnotherapist and pre-recorded my own hypnosis sessions. I would really listen to them at night while going to sleep. After about three years, I began to put the pieces together and have been able to complete the entire image of my abduction. It's why I've gravitated to do such work in the first place. I've also spent many years working with others, some with cattle mutilations, others with post-traumatic stress disorder related to alien abduction. There's no doubt in my mind that there is not only a correlation and causation to the possibility of why psychics always seem to have an abduction story of their own. So Sarah, I'll ask you again, *when* were you abducted?"

I was terribly interested to learn more about the cattle mutilations, I wanted to pick up and read all of his books almost immediately as to make the most of our interview. Instead, I learned quite quickly that the doctor had taken the authoritative role and I was no longer interviewing him for a paper. I described my childhood reoccurring dreams and some of my latent fears that I couldn't seem to rationalize.

"I bet we could do some work in a regression that would help you remember the experience. Like you said, I do not subscribe to coincidence and I bet you have poetry or scary tales of aliens somewhere in your childhood journal."

I could hear him sipping on his coffee between words and even though he was being quite general, his words spoke intently to the alien poetry I knew could be found in the binders I kept in my bedroom closet. He kept reiterating little discrepancies in a person's character or mannerisms and how they linked to abductions. He utilized a lot of psychological concepts to describe the connection. I was mystified, I was boggled, I was intrigued, and most importantly, I was terrified. Did I indeed have an experience with being abducted that I just couldn't remember?

A few weeks later I received a box in the mail from the doctor. It included a little black book of his networking colleagues and a few copies of his book that he himself had made highlights and underscores in. He'd included a handwritten note about his intrigue and excitement for my work; to know that after his death, people would continue on with research and that was what it was all about.

I coveted that box for quite some time, and was so thankful my professor had introduced me to the doctor that started my path down the research of the alien connection. After reading through the notes and research within the box, I found a home with a local community that had support groups and did research on UFO sightings. I attended conferences, I expanded my home library on the topic, and I began to keep an open eye out for regressions and experiences of those within my hypnotherapy community. Then I started having the dreams again.

Usually I went years between having scary dreams in the night; terrors that haunted me as a child had long since passed after my adolescence faded. Here I was, in my mid-twenties, and again having night terrors. I would wake up in the middle of the night unable to move as if I was a patient subdued by anesthetic but could still feel the pain and the fear. I never imagined myself or saw my body within a craft of some kind, surrounded by some sterile atmosphere, but it was real. I didn't empathize with many of the abduction stories I had read and researched. Instead I always felt trapped in my own room, as if my room was a hologram or simulation of some kind; intuitively I knew I wasn't safe and the room wasn't real.

Not only was I having night terrors, but I was also having a lot of stress and turbulence in my private life. I wrote off many of my nightmares to the fact that I was so stressed while awake. I was finishing my undergraduate degree and working with some very heinous clients and my marriage was failing. It had taken three invasive surgeries to determine that I was unable to bear children and my husband was losing interest in me after the news we would never have a family. My world was falling apart and at night I found no sanctuary. Everything was crumbling around me.

The night terrors continued after I did a short sale on my home and my divorce was finalized. The night terrors continued as I finished with clients having poltergeist experiences and also through investigations all over the country. I would wake up in Gettysburg in a cold sweat after having been paralyzed in my bed with fear for hours. A few weekends later I found myself in Birmingham, Alabama, at another event and again wishing I would have the insomnia I usually suffered from just to avoid the nightmares.

I couldn't always recall the detail, but usually it seemed as if I woke in terror and was paralyzed until the debilitation wore off and I jumped out of bed. There was almost always a time lapse between the time I woke up looking at the clock, unable to move, and the time in which I got up to run to the bathroom to splash my face with water. My life was on repeat and meaning was gone. It was not until one particular incident that I decided it wasn't a coincidence, and it wasn't just a response from high stress. There was something more going on.

I had been staying with some friends in Minneapolis, renting out the guest bedroom. The two girls were coworkers and friends of mine and the entire house looked like a showroom floor at a high-end furniture outlet. Everything had its place and everything was pristine. The two girls and I had a wonderful time in that house and I finally felt as if my life was starting to calm down, to turn around for the better. I had been accepted to my specialized graduate program, I was single and really enjoying my life, and I hadn't had a night terror in weeks.

I had decided to break out the old box the doctor had given me and leaf through some of the investigations he had. I was amazed at the correlation they were finding between nuclear power plants and cattle mutilations. I was also impressed with some of the hypnosis techniques the doctor was using to make sure anything and everything that was retrieved from the mind of the client was completely nonsuggestive. I went to bed that night listening to my music through headphones and hypothesizing about the future research I looked forward to doing.

This time I didn't awaken in the night paralyzed. For someone who's used to waking up around noon, working the night shift at the mental health hospital, I woke up with the sun on my day off. I had the ruminants of the night terror dripping from my thoughts, though I had not recalled the usual experience. I pulled my headphones from my ears and pulled my hands over my eyes, wiping away any hair that was brushed over my face. I took in a deep breath and exhaled... Whatever it was, it was over. I sat up in bed and threw my legs over the side to get up and stretch, as I do every morning. This time, when I stood up and arched my back, stretching my arms to the sky, a warm liquid rolled down my lower stomach, my upper thigh, and down my leg.

It was blood. It was my blood. At first, as every woman might unconsciously do, I thought I'd started my menstrual cycle and had a very inconvenient mess to deal with. I, however, hadn't had a menstrual cycle in years and wondered if I had scratched myself in my sleep. I followed the trail of blood up to its source and was surprised to see it was streaming out of my belly button. I didn't feel any pain, I didn't see any wound; blood was just coming out of my belly button. It was the strangest thing I'd ever seen.

I jumped into the shower and washed myself. Even after ten minutes, through the steam, I could see a river of pink flowing to the drain. I got out and dried off with the towel and watched myself in the mirror. Slowly, trickling blood began to drip from my belly button once again.

A Band-Aid wouldn't work, neither did gauze and tape, so I bunched up a washcloth and laid it over my belly button while wrapping my waist in a workout wrap for bench press. I had the day off, so I intended to eat breakfast and work around the house until taking note of my belly button again. I hated the doctor, and at this point didn't really connect any dots or find any coincidence in the fact I was bleeding in a strange way after just having had another unique dream.

Three hours later, I was still bleeding. I began to show it off like a circus sideshow act to my roommates, who were coming home from work. One of my roommates was convinced I must've scratched off a mole or nicked a scar because she had a scar on her chin that would bleed all day long if she reopened the wound. We all laughed at my inconvenience and enjoyed dinner. That night I had another dream.

This time I was consciously aware that I was dreaming and that I was also not attached to my physical body. Much like I had read about the experience of astral projection or someone who is hallucinating on a psychedelic drug, I felt a large sense of peace and detachment. I floated around the room until I was sucked out the window and awoke again in a new room. The room was very sterile, but I wasn't strapped down and I wasn't surrounded with strange alien figures, instead I was all alone. There was no noise, no intuitive feelings, no anything.

As I walked out of the room, noticing it had no doors, I was in some strange science fiction environment like you would see in a movie: sterile, cold, metallic. I almost began to consider the fact I was recollecting some scene from an '80s alien movie. I felt as though I was surrounded by hematite; cold and metallic everywhere. I was barefoot. I was lucid, I was conscious, and I was narrating my own dream. Just as I began to feel as though I was inside some sort of video game exploring for the sake of my own curiosity, I heard a noise of machines behind me. It startled me and I ran. The next thing I knew I was waking up in a cold sweat. I reached for my belly button, which was no longer bleeding. No scab, no blood, nothing.

The next day I couldn't keep my mind off of that dream. It seemed familiar to me, but it didn't seem like the piece of the memory from a movie or film. It definitely wasn't something that I had created in my mind because I had felt so unsafe, and I didn't know if the timing of the dream was a coincidence or not.

Coincidently, that lunch hour, I received a unique e-mail from a high school teacher who had found me online. Apparently my high school was doing an "our graduates" series and an English professor of mine was curious to see where I had been in life. She had googled my name, followed my website, and was sending me an e-mail. "I always remember thinking you'd be the next Stephen King of your generation!"

Attached to the e-mail were a few scanned items from my assignments she had kept over the years. One was a short story. As I read it, I remembered the short story and the assignment quite well. The teacher had been teaching a creative writing course, which challenged us to write something that consisted of twenty-six sentences, wherein each sentence began with the letter of the alphabet in order. It read:

Aftermath is what I was looking at, but from what
… I did not know. Be wilted and confused I stood,
wondering just where I was. Casted metallic shadows
swirled on the cold iron-like floor beneath me, and a
silent humming was swimming deep within my ears.
Disoriented, I looked down at my own self and poor in
shock; what had I become? Engravings of doings, not
my own, had mutilated my once smooth flesh. Fresh
saturated and now sutured pulp of what used to be my
skin lay palpitating upon my bones; my mouth then
she stripped of its teeth no-show scabs in their absence
and tears of blood seeped from my pores like sweat.
God, what had happened to me! Horrified and lost, I
somehow did not feel a fear; I felt a sense of confusion
and a wanting to find answers. Immersing myself deeper
into the tunnel-like metal cord door, I began to see an
approaching light. Juggling thoughts of what might
be down that tunnel in front of me … I found myself
clasping onto a faint trickling noise. Killing all of my
thoughts of hope, I stared at what I was beginning to
see appear in front of me. Little dim figures grew clearer
in my vision as I began to approach closer; and then I
needed not come any closer at all, as I could now tell
what exactly it was I saw. Milky white bodies lie before
me and even though I knew I should help … I just could
not move. Nothing in all my life was ever to prepare me
for the site I was now gazing deeply upon, this devilish
act upon helpless human victims. Ominous quivers
in their pale bloodless flesh, the metal hooks hoisting
their warm flesh about their bodies told me none of us

here were safe; the people who did this act were still
here, if they were indeed people at all. Paralyzed as I
stared, I gazed over the human experiments' nearby
canisters of blood, also the tantalizing metal objects
that had decorated the victims carcasses. Quaintly, I
began to distinguish movement and myself once again
and wondered what I was to do. Ripping at my own
conscience I decided these tormented souls could
not be helped by me and I turned my back to leave.
Samples of their sour and deathly stench penetrated
my every breath in their bones, groans, and screams
for help lingered in my ears as I walked away. Tapering
thoughts of going back soon left my brain and I was
now focused on how to save myself... How to leave
this imprisonment. Underfed and half-desecrated, my
body faltered in response to my wanting to go faster,
and then despite all effort, I froze. Vacant tables like the
one I had seen before bearing the cadavers of faintly
living survivors now blocked the hallway before me;
they hadn't been here earlier. Whisperers echoed down
the long car door and jolted my breath among my lungs
I could see my own heart throbbing through my own
pale flesh. X-shaped burns upon my hands began to
sizzle and rip apart my veins and thin skin, and then a
computer-type figure appeared that I had not noticed
before upon the wall. Yelling in pain and agonizing
terror I fell to my knees before the chrome tables before
me that now seemed to be reflecting my very feet. Zero
hour was here upon my soul in the now alien figure
glaring and smirking at me assured me of just that.

This had been written by me nearly six years before the experience I had just woken up from, and quite honestly it terrified me. I wasn't sure what to think of the fact that I was now experiencing the strange encounters and it always seemed to happen after I was doing UFO research. Sure, I have had many experiences of believing I had seen something in the sky but nothing reached out and grabbed me; nothing was all that memorable. Nothing froze my car on the highway and beamed me up in a ball of light to a spacecraft in the sky. However, I was now waking up with marks on my body and blood I couldn't rationalize... What more of a sign of contact did I need?

I called the doctor and told him of my story. He repeated the same old phrase by Friedrich Nietzsche that I often remind my paranormal clients of:

"When you look into the abyss the abyss also looks into you."

I didn't want to admit that I could never go back and I definitely didn't want to believe that I was being taken from my bed at night and tested on. Truth of the matter is, how many coincidences make a fact? I was very young and had already been diagnosed with ovarian cancer, endometriosis, and polycystic ovarian disease, and had issues with menstruating. I had the anxiety, I fit the demographic, I had the curiosity, and I also had the night terrors. At that time, I completely refused to go under hypnosis and have a regression about my alien encounters. I'm still too scared. The truth is, if once you see them they really do see you, then I guess I am paranoid that the more I look for an answer the more I might just find one.

Conclusion

Everyone has a paranormal ghost story to tell. Sometimes there is a simple stream of light in a family photo or something that pulls you out of bed at night and drags you into the closet. I firmly believe that every horror movie writer or science fiction producer has had some personal connection to what the universal unconscious knows to be true; there is another side and it can be dark.

I believe that religions and early human civilizations have always drawn things in the sky and interacted with the spiritual realm, because it does exist. It's hard to measure and therefore we've had to learn of its existence through metaphorical tales and stories; legends and lore. Spiritual activity doesn't abide by the same rules that the physical world does, and it doesn't have to be measured in a quantity. It happens in the daytime, and it happens at three o'clock at night. Most importantly, it happens even when we're not paying attention. Synchronicity or not, if you do begin to see the signs and listen to the stories and consider that every cave drawing of a dot in the sky wasn't just a star or planet, you'll realize it might indeed be something that's helped us along.

Why is it so far-fetched from a tale of a man living in the sky that we call God sending down His son to die for our sins? Some of the religious stories, many of the prophets, and the tales that we choose to believe in an edited Bible include stories that defy the laws of physics in nature. Yet the masses accept them and refute the paranormal. Men walking on water, talking snakes, and the resurrection of the physical body by the power of the spirit. I don't know if I completely agree with what religions are trying to teach and I definitely can't place a guarantee on all of my paranormal experiences or encounters.

What I do know is that the stories I've shared with you are just a handful of some of the experiences I've had throughout my life. The more I pay attention, the less I skeptically deduce everything to being chance. The more I pay attention, the more I gain in knowledge. I still remain skeptical and I still question everything, but my scope of realism doesn't just stop between what can and cannot happen via the laws of physics.

For those who are absolutely desperate to experience something within the paranormal because the skeptic in them simply cannot accept that such magical things exist, I tell you this: You are now a part of my story.

It reminds me of this old 1980s movie about a little boy reading into a magical tale for which he becomes a part of. Just as quantum mechanics would validate the importance of the observer in any known experiment, my life is my experiment and you the reader have just made it real. The story is growing, the legacy continues, and the energy shifted a little bit in the universe.

For those of us who have had a paranormal experience, these stories can simply validate what you may have already experienced in your life. Everyone's journey is different, but sometimes the evil of the world, even in the spiritual realm, looks the same to most of us. When you are reading through the pages of this book, you are on the journey with me and those entities and energies transfer to you. Look over your shoulder, and make sure no one's there. Or is there?

One of the Sinti traditions of spirituality is the battle being fought in a spiritual underworld; the dualities we see in everyday life: man and woman, light and dark, bad and good, Yin and Yang, positive and negative. We also know this duality extends to the spiritual realm. Angels and demons, fairies and trolls, the moon and the sun...they are all keeping a great balance in the world. Religions often use a greater power or authority in order to expel energy from one place (the person or thing it is possessing) to somewhere else.

An exorcism, for example, uses the graces of God and faith to put forth ritual and intent that believes the spirit will move on. Sometimes it does, sometimes it doesn't. The gypsy tradition of the Sinti people is to intentionally pass on the energy.

If you have a haunted item, then you must give it away. If you have a curse that cannot be broken, then you must curse someone else. It's almost as if it's a reflection of karma.

Either way, my story is with you now, and in some way, I suppose for those things that have lingered in the abyss with me might now have moved on. They are now lingering with you.

An Open Mind

Cryptozoology is not just about the chupacabra or Bigfoot and instead is simply about discovering unclassified animals, and we find new species every day. Ufology and the study of UFOs and alien abduction is not just about following up with clients that may or may not be struggling with mental illness, but also includes the quantitative research of cattle mutilations, time loss, time slips, and even mystical occurrences like that which happen in the Bermuda triangle. The paranormal does not just deal with haunted buildings and bumps in the night. The paranormal and the research of the paranormal includes anything that doesn't happen on the normal spectrum, which can be many things.

I hope if someone experiencing paranormal activity gets the opportunity to read my stories in this book that they, too, will understand that maybe what's happening to them is not a delusion, it's not a mental illness, and it's nothing to be immediately fearful of. Rather, it's something that should be taken seriously.

Know yourself, know your limits, and know that the world around you has no limits. How far do you want to go down this rabbit hole ... ?